# SIMPLE
# stenciling
## DRAMATIC QUILTS

85 Full-Size Stencil Patterns
6 Projects

Pam Stallebrass

C&T PUBLISHING

Text © 2007 Pam Stallebrass

Artwork © 2007 Pam Stallebrass and C&T Publishing, Inc.

PUBLISHER: Amy Marson

EDITORIAL DIRECTOR: Gailen Runge

ACQUISITIONS EDITOR: Jan Grigsby

EDITOR: Liz Aneloski

TECHNICAL EDITORS: Helen Frost and Nanette S. Zeller

COPYEDITOR/PROOFREADER: Wordfirm Inc.

COVER DESIGNER: Kristy K. Zacharias

DESIGN DIRECTOR/BOOK DESIGNER: Rose Sheifer

ILLUSTRATOR: Richard Sheppard

PRODUCTION COORDINATOR: Zinnia Heinzmann

QUILT PHOTOGRAPHY: Alain Proust, unless otherwise noted

HOW-TO PHOTOGRAPHY: Luke Mulks

Published by C&T Publishing, Inc., P.O. Box 1456, Lafayette, CA 94549

Front cover: *Nymph of the Evergreen Woodland*

Library of Congress Cataloging-in-Publication Data

Stallebrass, Pam.
  Simple stenciling-dramatic quilts : 85 full-size stencil patterns, 6
projects / Pam Stallebrass.
    p. cm.
  ISBN-13: 978-1-57120-325-0 (paper trade : alk. paper)
  ISBN-10: 1-57120-325-7 (paper trade : alk. paper)
  1. Stencil work. 2. Quilting. I. Title.

TT270.S773 2007
746.46--dc22

                    2006021836

Printed in China
10 9 8 7 6 5 4 3 2 1

## Dedication

To Linda, Matthew, and Madelin

## Acknowledgments

Quilters have been unbelievably kind in helping me get the projects ready for this book. Jean Thomas, Des van Niekerk, Ashley Germani, Pat Thorne, Martie McLea, Nohleen Berkman, Lorraine Bodie, and Beverley Patterson all helped me quietly and graciously.

My editor at C&T publishing, Liz Aneloski, has patiently stood by me.

Thanks to Judith Appio for so kindly and generously allowing me to photograph the Nigerian stencil and indigo cloths at her exhibition. Thanks to John Gillow for allowing me to use his beautiful quilt from Pakistan.

Thanks to Alain Proust and Peter Steltzman for photographing the quilts and Heather Scott for allowing me to photograph some of the quilts in her garden.

Thank you Dianne Huck for allowing me to show two of the quilts used in articles in *British Patchwork and Quilting*, and Vicki Jensen at PRO Chem who was really helpful in supplying paints for photography.

Roxanne Peters at the Victoria and Albert Museum in London and Maureen Robinson from David Bateman Publishers in New Zealand both provided me with wonderful photographs for the chapter on stencils around the world.

A special thanks to Joe and Matthew for their patience while every surface in the house was covered with quilting paraphernalia.

# CONTENTS

## PROJECTS

A stencil, template, or mask can be used in numerous ways to help you create beautiful and unusual fabric for your quiltmaking.

A stencil is anything that prevents color from reaching selected areas of the fabric, thus creating a pattern. It can be a purchased stencil made from clear plastic, or your own design cut from an X-ray plate or freezer paper. It can even be a found object, like the leaves I used in the quilt for the first project (page 20).

Very little equipment is needed to stencil, and it can be done in the kitchen or on the dining room table. Even though the process is extremely easy, the results can be as complex and beautiful as you wish to make them.

There are many ways to stencil and dye fabrics. This book just provides a stepping-off point. As you experiment, you will discover ways that are easier for you. Enjoy the process. There are no right or wrong ways to stencil. It is the results that matter. You just have to start. It doesn't matter if your first effort isn't so great; it will lead to something else. The first steps may be a challenge, but very soon you will get the hang of the technique and discover a whole new source of creativity within yourself.

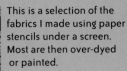

This is a selection of the fabrics I made using paper stencils under a screen. Most are then over-dyed or painted.

## Stencils Around the World

Stencils make it quick and easy to repeat designs on a piece of fabric. As a means of decorating fabric, stenciling has been used throughout the world for hundreds of years. Color was either applied directly through the stencil, or a resist of the local starch—rice in Japan or cassava in Nigeria—was applied through the stencil, and after drying the fabric was placed in a dye bath, usually indigo.

In Nigeria, West Africa, the designs on *adire* cloths are made by pressing a paste, made from cassava, through a metal stencil, and when the fabric is dry it is dyed in indigo. Foil from the inside of tea boxes used to be the stencil material; now zinc sheets are used.

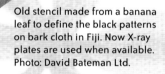

Old stencil made from a banana leaf to define the black patterns on bark cloth in Fiji. Now X-ray plates are used when available. Photo: David Bateman Ltd.

Designs on *adire* cloth from Nigeria. The writing translates as "There is no king but God." (Collection of Judith Appio.)

A bark cloth, or *masi kesa*, from Fiji decorated with stenciled designs. Photo: David Bateman Ltd.

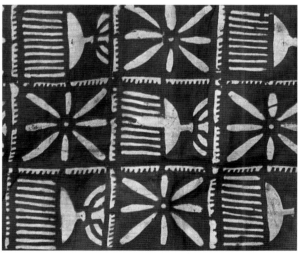

Resist stencil designs on adire cloth from Nigeria, known as Comb and Flower. (Collection of Judith Appio.)

A modern Japanese kimono, *Flight*, by Matsubara Yoshichi, 1990. In a process known as *katazome*, rice paste was applied to the fabric as a resist (to stop the dye from reaching that part of the fabric). The largest stencil was used first, then the fabric was dyed in indigo. This process was repeated with all 29 stencils, which become successively smaller, creating a wonderfully subtle design. The multiple dippings in indigo produce a rich, vibrant blue.

Two modern pieces of stenciled fabric from China

Stenciled quilts and bedcoverings were made from about 1820 to 1850 in New England and New York. The same theorems or stencils that were used by young ladies at school were used to decorate quilts. Concentrated vegetable dye or store-bought pigments were mixed with gum arabic and applied to the fabric with a brush or pad of cloth. Detail was added later with a brush.

The Japanese are masters in the art of stencil making. See how the bubbles hold the long thin strips securely, and the scales on the body of the fish form a continuous pattern. There are no loose pieces or large undecorated spaces. It is cut from two sheets of mulberry paper. (Collection of the Victoria and Albert Museum, London.)

A zinc stencil from Abeokuto, Nigeria. The local starch, cassava, is made into a paste and spread over the stencil onto the fabric. When dry, it is dyed in indigo. (Collection of Judith Appio.)

The choice of fabrics available to the modern quilter is awe-inspiring—sometimes rather overwhelming.

I use the seasons to help group certain colors together. The spring colors are uncomplicated and fresh: the primary and secondary colors. The summer colors are a little more complicated: tertiary colors made by mixing a primary and a secondary color, or two secondary colors. In the autumn the colors are strong, warm, matured tertiaries. In the winter colors become less intense and sometimes paler, but they are still complex.

## Spring

Spring colors are the fresh primary and secondary colors we see in the color wheel. The new leaves that grow on the skeletal winter trees are soft and fresh and new. The first flowers that open, such as the daffodils, are bright and clear.

*The Green Oak* (page 55) uses greens mixed with blue and a lemon yellow.

The greens in *Tree of Life* (page 56) are mixed with blue and a golden yellow.

*Elephant Bag* (page 26) uses only yellow, orange, and red.

*Spring* (page 60) was made using primary (blue, red, and yellow) and secondary (purple, green, and orange) colors. It has a fresh, bright appeal.

## Summer

In summer the colors mature and become more complex. A mixture of cool and warm colors, these tertiary colors are made by combining a primary and secondary color together, or two secondary colors. You achieve some really beautiful, unexpected colors this way.

In *Mandela's Gold* (page 59), purple and orange are mixed together to create a wonderful range of muted colors.

In *Nymph of the Evergreen Woodland* (page 49), the green-to-purple mix was used for some muted colors.

In *Agapanthus* (page 36), two secondary colors, purple and green, are mixed together in five different proportions to make a series of tertiary colors. These are strip pieced with purples and greens.

## Autumn

Blended colors (mixtures of three colors) are the colors I love and use most frequently. My yellows have touches of blue and red, my reds have additions of blue and yellow, and my blues have little bits of red and yellow to make strong jewel colors.

I can play with a color, altering the mix slightly to make it brighter or duller. Gold, maroon, purple, orange, and red are the main colors in this group.

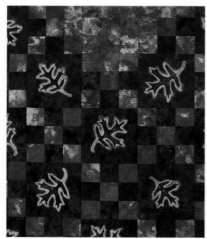

Light orange shaded autumn colors are offset by strong maroon in the Nine-Patch blocks of *Autumn Leaf Jacket* (page 55).

*Spirit of the Yellowwood* (page 53) uses my favorite autumn shades in the pieced blocks.

The black strip piecing in *Tropical Butterflies* (page 42) contrasts with the bright autumn colors in the triangles.

Detail of *The Veggie Patch* (page 54)

Lovely warm colors are used in *Bees and Elephants—Autumn Shades* (page 34).

## Winter

I have included blue and white, pastels, and metallics in the winter colors. These are still tertiary colors, even the blue. Since it has red and yellow mixed in with it to tone it down, it is subdued and cool.

I love indigo blue. Blue was probably the first colorfast color to be used on fabric. Many different indigo-bearing plants are found throughout the world, in tropical and temperate climates, and for thousands of years this wonderful color has been used to dye cloth. The complex dyeing method results in many different blues, from pale sky blue through the middle tones to almost black.

*Blue and White Leaves* (page 20)

The rich indigo blue of a resist-stencilled fabric from West Africa

Alternate colorway of *Agapanthus* with pearl-based fabric paints (page 36)

*Color* **9**

# Stenciling

Stenciling is ideal for creating your own personal designs on cloth, either for quilting or clothing.

Stencils are masks made to stop color from being applied to specific parts of the fabric. We use both positive and negative stencils in this book, but I got so confused about which was which that I decided to use the term *stencil* if it was a sheet of stencil material with a design cut out of it, and *template* if the part that was cut out was used.

Stencil

Template

## Stencil Materials

We can use an array of different materials for stencils. You don't have to try them all, but you should experiment a bit until you find one that you enjoy working with and that suits your purposes.

✦ **FREEZER PAPER** is readily available and reasonably priced. It is easy to cut with scissors or a craft knife and is temporarily fixed in place with an iron. It is thin, so the paint doesn't cake up on the cut edges or bleed underneath the stencil. Because freezer paper can be adhered to the fabric, it is possible to design stencils that are not held together with ties as in traditional stencils. You just arrange the separate pieces and iron them onto the fabric. This method can be fiddly when there are lots of loose pieces, and designs usually cannot be repeated exactly, but I think that is part of the charm of freezer-paper templates. They can be reused several times, but they do tend to distort after a while.

Cut several layers of freezer paper at a time. If the layers slip, staple them together. You can cut them with a pair of sharp scissors if you are not going to use the outside stencil later. If you want to keep the outside intact, use a sharp craft knife.

use an array
of different
materials for
stencils

✦ **TRANSPARENT STENCIL PLASTIC** is more durable than freezer paper and can be used if you need to repeat a design many times. It can be purchased at craft shops. X-ray plates (soak in bleach to remove the image), acetate, and overhead projector transparencies also work well. These materials can be cut with a craft knife or a heated stencil cutter. They are easy to line up to add multiple colors. These stencils can be temporarily held in place while working with repositionable glue, such as Bostik Fast-Tak. When cutting designs in these materials you need to make sure that all the various pieces are connected to the main part of the stencil with ties. (See Lesotho horseman, below.)

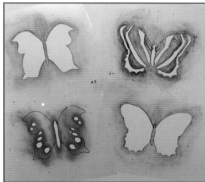

Butterfly stencils

Leaf template

✦ **FOUND OBJECTS**, such as leaves, make great stencils and templates. I used real leaves for the first project, gluing each leaf down and stenciling a halo around it. Leaves are also fun for sun prints, which I love using on the backs of quilts.

✦ **COMPUTER PAPER** works well if you are printing stencils under a screen. It is also suitable for making quilting templates.

I use paper stencils for many of the fabrics I print. I cut my designs from computer paper, lay them on the fabric, and print over them with a flat or rotary screen. I usually use thickened Procion dyes, and I can print about 40 yards with the same stencils. The stencils may take a long time to cut, but the materials are very inexpensive, which allows you to experiment. If it works, wonderful, and if it's a flop, it's not the end of the world!

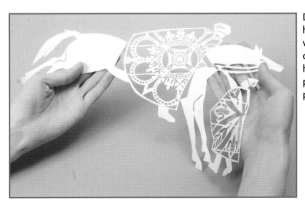

Detail of Lesotho horseman. This stencil was cut from paper. My challenge was to make it hold together in one piece (with ties) when I picked it up.

✦ **MASKING TAPE**, available in various widths, works wonderfully for making stripes.

Green stripe made using masking tape

Different widths of masking tape

## General Materials and Equipment

You will need the following tools and materials.

✦ Your craft knife is one of your most important tools. I like one that has a pencil-thin handle. Keep the blade sharp by rubbing it periodically on a piece of very fine sandpaper or emery board. When it starts tearing the stencil instead of cutting, change the blade.

✦ Most quilters have self-healing mats for rotary cutting. These mats are perfect for cutting stencils on.

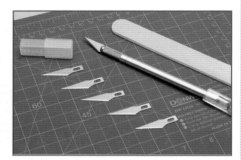

Cutting knife, spare blades, sandpaper, and self-healing cutting board

✦ You will need tracing paper and a fine black pen or pencil for tracing. If you are tracing directly onto acetate, look for a pen that draws on film, such as a permanent marker.

✦ Transparent tape or masking tape.

✦ I like ½″ and ¼″ stenciling brushes and square watercolor brushes. Using the smaller one takes longer, but it gives finer detail. Sponge rollers are useful for large areas.

✦ Old plates and small glass bottles for mixing paints.

✦ Sometimes a flat surface is fine for printing on, but if the fabric is a bit thin the paint seeps under the stencil. I have a sheet of Perspex (clear plastic sheeting) that easily holds a fat quarter, and I have stretched a double layer of T-shirt material over it and fixed it with masking tape on the back. It is a lovely surface to print on, and it soaks up any paint that goes through the fabric I am printing.

✦ Inks and paints are dealt with in the Paints, Dyes, and Paint Sticks chapter beginning on page 16.

✦ A domestic iron to set the fabric paints.

✦ Drawing equipment: pencils, erasers, and rulers.

✦ Repositionable spray adhesive to attach stencils to fabric.

## Making the Stencil

The stencil is the shape of your design. Don't rush; spend time drawing or tracing your design and then cutting it out.

**1.** Trace or draw the design. If you are using acetate, use a permanent fine-point pen. After you have traced the design, write the name of the project on the stencil. This is especially important when you are using acetate, since it also tells you which is the right side of the stencil.

**2.** Simple designs can be cut with scissors. Most designs, however, must be cut with a craft knife. Use a sharp blade, and cut on a self-healing mat. You might find it easier to rotate the stencil rather than moving your hand. Keep your fingers out of the way, especially the hand that is holding the stencil down. Those little knives are very sharp. Start by cutting the little pieces out of the stencil.

**3. If you make a mistake** and cut out the wrong piece on an acetate or film stencil, tape the piece back on. If this happens with freezer paper, cut a patch from freezer paper a bit larger than the hole, and iron it on. It works like a charm.

## Preparing the Fabric

**1.** Choose a fabric.

Fiber content is not critical for fabric paints, since they will be fine on fabric that is only 50% cotton, but if you are using thickened dyes, make sure you use 100% cotton fabric.

**2.** Prewash the fabric.

Sometimes fabric shrinks after you print the first stencil, and there is a problem fitting the second on top. You can avoid this problem by washing your fabric in hot water before beginning.

Fabrics are usually treated with sizing agents, which have to be removed before you stencil. For hand washing, add ¼ teaspoon Synthrapol to 1 gallon (4 liters) of hot (140°F/60°C) water; for machine washing use 2 tablespoons of Synthrapol and wash on a hot cycle. Synthrapol is a cleaning agent that you can buy from dye suppliers.

It is possible to buy cotton that is prepared for dyeing (PFD) or prepared for printing (PFP). You can use these without prewashing.

**3.** Iron the fabric well, since crinkles will make it difficult to make an even print.

**4.** Cut the fabric to the size required by the design. It is safer to start with your fabric about 1″ larger all around. After stenciling and ironing, it can be trimmed to its final size.

## Printing the Stencil

**1.** Adhere the stencil to the fabric.

If you are using a stencil made from film or acetate, spray the back of the stencil with a repositionable adhesive. Hold the spray can at least 18″ away, and spray lightly. Position the stencil in the center of your fabric and press it down with your hand. The glue must be removed with mineral turpentine and a rag when it is no longer tacky.

If you are using freezer paper, position the cut stencil in the center of your fabric, then iron in place with a **dry** iron. Press firmly, making sure the stencil has adhered all over.

**2.** Use whatever feels easiest to apply the paint over your stencil. A stencil brush is easy to use. Don't use too much paint at a time or it will seep under the stencil. Pounce the paint on in a series of up and down bounces keeping the brush vertical. A few pounces give a broken texture, which can be nice for certain subjects. The addition of more paint gives a more solid color. A wide, square watercolor brush, a makeup sponge, a sponge roller, or a sea sponge (for an interesting texture) can also be used.

Printing stencil with stencil brush

Painting over stencil with watercolor brush

Using a sponge roller

A screen used for screen-printing can be placed over the stencil and printed with a squeegee.

A screen placed over a paper stencil means you can quickly make multiple prints.

Squeeze bottles are used to apply the light-sensitive paint to the fabrics before a sun print.

Squeezing different colors onto a piece of cloth before placing the leaves on it for a sun print

**3.** Fabric paint and Markal Paintstiks are the easiest to use, but it is also possible to use thickened Procion dyes (page 18).

**4.** To add detail to your stenciling, leave the stencil in place and paint another layer of color with a finer brush, as in the *Agapanthus* quilt.

**5.** More than one stencil can be used to add detail or extra colors. Cut 2 stencils and print the detail on top of the first color, as in *Tropical Butterflies* (page 42).

Detail of *Agapanthus* quilt (page 36)

First stencil

Second stencil

**6.** Additional colors can also be added freehand with a paintbrush, as in *The Veggie Patch* (page 54).

A freezer-paper stencil was used to apply the black background. After drying and ironing, color was added with a paintbrush and fabric paint.

**7.** When removing the freezer-paper stencil, place the fabric and stencil face down on a firm surface. Lift the corner of the fabric and pull it off the stencil. If you pull the stencil off from the front it curls up and is difficult to reuse.

### Making Sun Prints

Work outside in the sun when painting large pieces of fabric; smaller pieces can be prepared on a board and carried outside.

**1.** Wet the fabric and squeeze out as much water as possible. Paint the fabric with light-sensitive paint.

**2.** Place the items to be printed onto the fabric. Place in the sun and let dry. Where the items cover the fabric the color will be light, and where the sun reaches the fabric the color will be dark. The brighter the sun, the crisper the images.

## Curing or Heat Setting

### Fabric Paints

Fabric paints are not washable until they have been heat set. This can be done in a number of ways. Ironing is the easiest. I have an Elnapress that I always use. The heat is even, and each piece takes about 12 seconds to cure. You can also place the fabric in a tumble dryer for 45 minutes on the hottest setting. It's possible to heat set the paint in your oven at 320°F (160°C), but turn the oven off before you put the fabric in or it may scorch.

### Thickened Procion Dyes

Procion dyes don't need to be heat set, but are cured by soda ash and time. They must be covered with a sheet of plastic because the chemicals must remain damp to be effective. I leave painted stenciling for 24 hours before washing.

Reactive dyes need to be rinsed very well to remove the excess dye that has not reacted with the fibers. Use ¼ teaspoon (1.25ml) of Synthrapol for every yard of fabric, and wash at 140°F (60°C). Rinse until the water runs clear.

## Trimming Stenciled Fabric

It is important to center the design in the block. I make a frame the size of the finished block plus seam allowance. I place this over the finished stencil and mark it with a pencil or chalk marker. Then I trim it, double-checking to be sure everything is square and the measurements are correct.

Using a frame to center the finished stenciled design

work outside in the sun

There are many ways to add color to your fabric using a stencil. They all produce slightly different results, but your choice will really be based on what technique you feel most comfortable using and how much space you have to work in.

## PAINTS VERSUS DYES

| | Paints | Dyes |
|---|---|---|
| Ease of Use | Very easy to use—out of the bottle, onto your fabric. | Thickener and dye solutions and fixer must be mixed and tested for color. |
| Availability | Readily available at any craft shop. | Available at specialist dye suppliers. |
| Permanence | Quick and easy to heat set with a domestic iron. | Must be kept damp and cured for 12 to 24 hours at over 68°F (20°C). |
| Fabric Hand | The emulsion that holds the color (pigment) in fabric paints coats the fibers and stays in the fabric, making it feel a little stiff, especially when opaque paints are used. | The thickener used with dyes is washed out after curing, leaving the fabric feeling exactly as it did before the color was added. |
| Color | Easy to see the final color; the paint is darker when wet, but you can dry it with a hair dryer and iron the fabric to check the color. | The colors look very dark when you paint them on, and it is best to cure and wash the dye to judge the final color before starting a big project. Curing takes 12 to 24 hours, so you can see that this is a lengthy process. |
| Fabric Content | Colorfast on cottons or synthetic blends. (Be careful not to melt the fabric when heat setting if you are using synthetic fabric.) | Can be used only on natural fibers, such as cotton, viscose, and linen. |
| Color Durability | The paints lie on the surface of the fabric, so when rubbed by wear or in the washing machine, fine lines become paler where the paint is rubbed off; this is known as crocking. You really only notice this on large areas of color. | Procion dyes, when cured, can be washed on the hot cycle in your machine for years and the colors will stay bright and clear. |

## Paints

Most craft shops stock paints at a reasonable price, and for stenciling you need only small quantities. Read your particular paint's instructions. Always do a wash test on the heat-set fabrics to establish that your painted fabric is washable.

The base or emulsion that holds the color can be **transparent, opaque,** or **pearl.** I buy the three bases and four pigments—lemon yellow, magenta, cyan (turquoise-blue), and black—so I can mix my own colors from scratch.

I buy the pigments (turquoise, yellow, and magenta) and the three different bases (transparent, opaque, and pearl) separately.

It is also possible to buy primary colors already mixed, but make sure you also have some unpigmented base to lighten your colors.

**Transparent fabric paints** are really easy to use, and as long as they are not applied too thickly they won't affect the hand (stiffness) of the fabric much. They are made up of a clear base, also known as an emulsion, with pigment (color) added. I would recommend lemon yellow, magenta, cyan (turquoise-blue), and black. Use a clear base to lighten your colors. If you add water it will make your paints too runny. These paints are transparent, like watercolors; if applied over another color or onto a colored fabric, the final color will be affected by the underlying color.

Transparent paint used in the *Agapanthus* quilt (page 36)

**Opaque fabric paints** are used on dark fabrics and have to be applied quite thickly. They are very effective but make the fabric feel stiff.

Lovely stenciled rose design by Alet Pieterse. Opaque and transparent inks were used on orange fabric.

**Pearl-based fabric paints** can be mixed into softly glowing golds, silvers, bronzes, coppers, and other colors.

Monoprint using pearl-based fabric paints

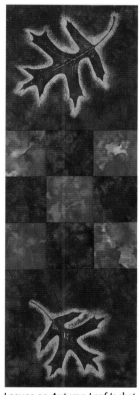

Leaves on *Autumn Leaf Jacket* (page 55) using pearl-based fabric paints

**Light-sensitive paints** can be used with leaves or black plastic as stencils or templates to make sun prints.

## Dyes

**Procion MX dyes** are ideal for the home dyer. They are fast reacting, easy to use, and available in small quantities in a wide range of colors from specialist craft shops and via the Internet. They are cold-water reactive dyes, curing at between 68°F and 104°F (20°C and 40°C), and need soda ash and time to fix the color to the fabric. The dye molecule reacts with the fiber molecule to become a part of the fiber. Only natural fibers, such as cotton, viscose, and silk, will react with the dyes.

Thickened Procion MX dyes leave the fabric just as soft as it was originally, and the colors are strong and clear and very colorfast. There are some disadvantages, though: the whole process takes a lot longer than coloring with fabric paints, and without a bit of experimenting you are not quite sure what the exact color will be after the final rinse. The thickener for reactive dyes is made from urea and sodium alginate. Ready-mixed thickeners can be purchased from dye suppliers. PRO Chemical makes one called PRO Thick SH.

I recommend that you buy only the primary colors, partly because of expense, but more importantly because it gives you more control over your color mixing. I use Blue MX R, Red MX 8B, and Yellow MX 3R as my usual palette. My extra colors are Yellow MX 4G (a lemon yellow), Turquoise 4G, and black.

When I first started using dyes I thought I would have to have an expensive scale. I went out and bought a medium-priced one, and it couldn't tell the difference between one and two teaspoons, so it was useless. I know scales have become a lot more accurate and affordable since then, but I am still happy measuring with teaspoons. Wear a dust mask and gloves when handling dry dyes and powders.

To measure an accurate teaspoon, scoop a teaspoon into the dye, then wipe the straight edge of a knife across the top.

If you want a fraction of a teaspoon, tip a teaspoon of dye onto a clean piece of paper, and with a knife divide it into two, then four, until you achieve your desired amount.

## Paint Sticks

These are oil-based crayons suitable for many surfaces. Lovely soft effects can be attained with these paint sticks, and they leave such a thin layer of paint that the fabric remains soft. The colors can be mixed on a plastic surface before they are applied with a stencil brush, or different colors can be overlaid, creating interesting results. Leave for three days, then iron to set the color.

A sun print made using a black plastic template

# Leaves

I found an oak leaf with a wonderfully asymmetrical shape on my daily walk. I placed it right side up on a piece of white muslin and, using a stencil brush, shaded the fabric paint from dark, near the leaf, to light. It looked crisp and lovely, but the inside looked a bit white. So I painted the back of the leaf and pressed it back onto the stenciled shape, and I got a faint impression of the leaf's veins. This would work!

The search is now on for leaves with interesting shapes. They have to be flat and fairly firm; judicious pruning will eliminate overlapping leaves.

I am continually amazed at the variety of leaf shapes and colors. I bring them home and store them between the pages of old telephone books until I am ready to use them.

The potential for leaves as stencils is limitless. Even all those people who think they can't draw can have lots of fun with these stencils.

# Blue and White Leaves

Designed, dyed, stenciled, and pieced by Pam Stallebrass, hand quilted by Jean Thomas, and bound by Ashley Germani. Photo by Peter Steltzman.

I decided to use a simple color scheme, blue and white, combined with Nine-Patch piecing, so even beginners will be tempted to give it a try.

I really hope you will go out and collect leaves to use as stencils. Choose leaves that are fairly stiff. I thought a maidenhair fern would look wonderful, but it was too soft and stuck to the fabric. Look for leaves with interesting shapes and different sizes. You can always use a whole group of smaller leaves. I have included patterns of a few leaf shapes that I have used (pages 78–80), including the bracken border (page 80), in case you can't find any in your neighborhood.

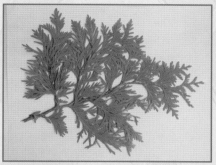 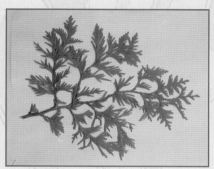

A bit of judicious pruning gives a better outline for stenciling.

- Quilt size: 74″ × 89″

- Block size: 7½″ × 7½″

- Borders: 2½″ and 8″

- Stencil method: Found objects, or templates from freezer paper or stencil plastic, and paint

Please read the Stenciling (pages 10–15) and Paints, Dyes, and Paint Sticks chapters (pages 16–18).

## Materials and Supplies

*Fabric requirements are based on 42″ fabric width. See pages 10–12 for more information on supplies.*

- 6 yards of white for the stenciled leaf blocks and border and Nine-Patch blocks

- ¾ yard each of 5 different blues (medium to dark) for the Nine-Patch blocks and inner border

- ¾ yard of blue for binding

- Batting: 78″ × 93″

- Backing: 78″ × 93″

- Real leaves, or freezer paper or stencil plastic

- Spray adhesive

- Fabric paints: Blue, red, yellow, and clear base to lighten the colors

- Stencil brush, ¼″ to ½″ in diameter

## Stenciling

### Cutting Fabric to Stencil

*The stenciled pieces will be trimmed to size before sewing. Extra width and length have been allowed.*

#### WHITE

✦ Cut 8 strips 10″ × the fabric width, then cut into 31 squares 10″ × 10″ for the leaf blocks. A few extras are useful, so you have a choice of leaves when you begin to put your quilt top together.

✦ Cut 4 strips 9″ × 75″ long for the border.

## Printing the Template

### LEAF BLOCKS

**1.** Draw squares $7\frac{1}{2}'' \times 7\frac{1}{2}''$, very lightly in pencil, on the 10″ white squares.

**2.** Mix a little bit of red and yellow into your blue paint—approximately 6 parts blue, $\frac{1}{2}$ part red, and $\frac{1}{2}$ part yellow. If it is too dark, add some clear base. Make a test print, let it dry, and iron it to see if it is the color you are looking for.

**3.** Use real leaves or trace the patterns (pages 78–80). Spray the backs of real leaves with adhesive or press freezer-paper templates in place with a hot iron. Stencil the leaves on the white squares by painting a halo around each leaf.

**4.** Wipe a little paint onto the leaf veins with a small, square-ended brush, then place it onto your stenciled leaf shape and press down with your fingers. These fine marks add interest and will be a guide for quilting later.

 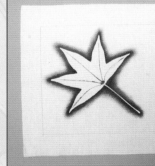

Wipe paint on back of leaf's veins.          Press down.

**5.** Heat set following the instructions on page 15.

**6.** Trim the blocks to $8'' \times 8''$.

### BORDER

**1.** Mark the final size of your border ($8'' \times 73\frac{1}{2}''$ for the top and bottom borders and $8'' \times 72\frac{1}{2}''$ for the sides) with small pencil marks on each of the border strips. Mark the width of each leaf with small pencil marks, leaving space between them (16 for the top and bottom with the 2 outside leaves at an angle to turn the corner, and 17 for the sides).

**2.** Stencil the border leaves, except for the 4 corner leaves. These will be stenciled after the borders are added to the quilt top.

**3.** Trim the top and bottom borders to $8\frac{1}{2}'' \times 74''$ and the sides to $8\frac{1}{2}'' \times 73''$.

The leaf in the corner is set at an angle. Stencil these after adding the border.

# Nine-Patch Blocks and Inner Border

## Cutting

### BLUE

✦ Cut 23 strips 3″ × the fabric width for the Nine-Patch blocks.

✦ Cut 7 strips 3″ × the fabric width for the inner borders. Cut into squares 3″ × 3″.

### WHITE

✦ Cut 13 strips 3″ × the fabric width for the Nine-Patch blocks.

✦ Cut 2 strips 3″ × the fabric width for the inner borders. Cut into squares 3″ × 3″.

## Nine-Patch Blocks

Sew the strips into the following sets. Make 2 of each set for the center Nine-Patch blocks. Make 1 of each set for the side and corner Nine-Patch blocks.

## Inner Border

Arrange and stitch the blue and white 3″ squares together—27 for each side inner border and 23 for the top and bottom inner borders.

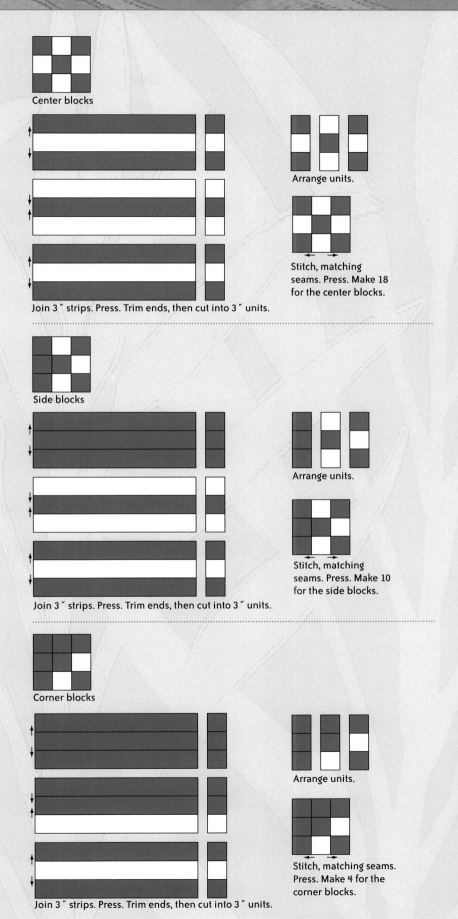

Center blocks

Join 3″ strips. Press. Trim ends, then cut into 3″ units.

Arrange units.

Stitch, matching seams. Press. Make 18 for the center blocks.

Side blocks

Join 3″ strips. Press. Trim ends, then cut into 3″ units.

Arrange units.

Stitch, matching seams. Press. Make 10 for the side blocks.

Corner blocks

Join 3″ strips. Press. Trim ends, then cut into 3″ units.

Arrange units.

Stitch, matching seams. Press. Make 4 for the corner blocks.

## Assembling the Quilt Top

1. Referring to the diagram, arrange and join the Nine-Patch and stencil blocks.

2. Add the side inner borders and press. Add the top and bottom inner borders and press.

3. And the side stenciled borders and press. Add the top and bottom stenciled borders and press.

4. Stencil the corner leaves.

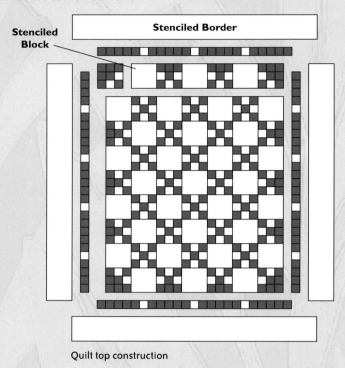

Quilt top construction

## Finishing

Layer, baste, and quilt.

Jean Thomas's hand quilting has turned a very simple design into an heirloom. She stitched around the outside of the leaves, then ¼ ˝ in from the blue squares, then quilted a diagonal lattice at ½ ˝ intervals.

The leaves in the border were quilted along the central stalk and along the veins, then the background was quilted in a diagonal lattice at 1 ˝ intervals.

For machine quilting ideas, see *Autumn Leaf Jacket* (page 55).

Bind with blue fabric (pages 61–62).

Detail of hand quilting (blocks)

# Bags

The elephants on this bag were inspired by rock paintings by the San (Bushmen). I love the simplicity of the shape that captures the essence of an elephant.

Use the patterns (page 66) or draw your own silly birds. Try cutting an imaginary head, body, wings, tail, and feet from separate pieces of white paper. Arrange them on a dark piece of paper until you are happy with your silly bird, then glue it down. Trace this shape onto freezer paper to make your template. After stenciling the background and adding color to the designs by hand, embroidery, beads, and sequins can be added.

I saw a picture of a square-based drawstring bag in Amy Katoh's lovely book *Blue and White Japan*. These bags were used by the country folk to carry anything from rice to coins. My daughter, Linda, made a pattern for me, and it is such a useful shape.

Designed, stenciled, painted, pieced, and quilted by Pam Stallebrass.

- Bag base: 8½″ × 8½″ finished

- Bag height: 11½″

- Stencil method: Templates from freezer paper and painted details

- Please read the chapters on Stenciling (pages 10–15) and Paints, Dyes, and Paint Sticks (pages 16–18).

## Materials and Supplies

*Fabric requirements are based on 42″ fabric width. See pages 10–12 for more information on supplies.*

- ½ yard of white for the stenciled area

- ⅓ yard of black for the base and drawstring casing

- ⅝ yard for lining

- 3 yards soft cotton cord for the drawstring

- Batting: 46″ × 12″

- Freezer paper

- Fabric paints: Black for the background and magenta, yellow, and clear base to color the elephants

- Stencil brush, ½″ in diameter, or foam roller for the background

- Small, firm watercolor brush for adding color to the elephants

## Stenciling

### Cutting Fabric to Stencil

**WHITE**

✦ Cut a rectangle 36″ × 12″ for the bag.

### Making the Templates

**1.** Trace the elephant pattern (page 65) onto freezer paper. If you want some of the elephants to face the opposite direction, place 2 pieces of freezer paper shiny side up and 2 pieces shiny side down. Make 12 elephant templates.

Cutting 4 layers of freezer paper. You can see the staples on the outside of the design holding the layers together.

**2.** Trace 4 stalks (page 65) onto freezer paper. Cut out. Cut 1 in half vertically.

**3.** There are 3 designs for the leaves (page 65). Trace a selection of leaves, layer several layers of freezer paper, and cut out. You will need about 70 leaves.

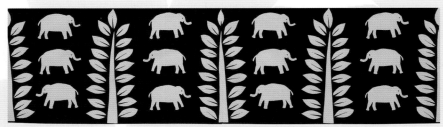

## Printing the Template

*See pages 13–14 for detailed instructions.*

**1.** Draw a pencil line to mark the print area, 34″ × 10″.

**2.** Place the half-stalk templates on the 10″ ends (when the seam is sewn it will create a whole stalk) and the whole-stalk templates evenly spaced in the center.

**3.** Position the leaves to look as if they are growing.

**4.** Place the elephants by referring to the photo.

Stencil placement

**5.** Press the templates in place with a hot iron.

**6.** Paint the print area with black paint.

**7.** Let dry, then peel off the stencils and iron the fabric to heat set the color. It is important to set the color before painting on the next colors because otherwise the black will smudge, dulling the applied colors.

## Painting the Elephants

**1.** Mix different amounts of magenta and yellow to make a series of oranges, lighten some with clear base.

The colors: yellow, orange, and red

**2.** The designs you could paint on each elephant are limitless. Some of the classics include stripes (horizontal, diagonal, or vertical), zigzags, wavy lines, blocks, or diamonds. Start with the palest color, since it acts as a resist. Wipe off any extra paint when you have finished, as thick fabric paint gets a bit rubbery and is difficult to quilt through.

**3.** When dry, iron to set the colors.

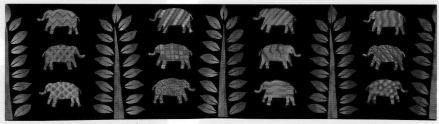

Quilt the bag before you sew it together.

## Assembling the Bag

### Cutting

✦ Trim the main bag piece to 34½″ × 10½″.

BLACK

✦ Cut 2 strips 19″ × 3½″ for the drawstring casing.

✦ Cut a square 9½″ × 9½″ for the base.

LINING

✦ Cut a piece 34½″ × 10½″ for the bag.

✦ Cut a piece 9″ × 9″ for the base.

BATTING

✦ Cut a square 8″ × 8″ for the base and 34″ × 10″ for the bag.

Detail of quilting

## Construction

**1.** Layer the bag and base pieces with the batting. Quilt the pieces before you sew them together.

Quilted base of bag. The concentric squares are drawn 1˝ apart.

**2.** Sew the 2 short sides of the bag together, right sides together, with a ¼˝ seam.

**3.** Starting at the seam, make tiny slits, just less than the ¼˝ seam allowance, 8½˝ apart around the bottom of the bag. These will make it easier to turn the corner when sewing.

**4.** Trim the base to 9˝ × 9˝. Sew the base to the bag one side at a time, lining up the four ¼˝ snips with the corners of the base.

Sew the base to the bag.

**5.** Repeat Steps 2–4 for the lining.

**6.** Turn the outer bag right side out and slip the lining in, so the wrong sides are facing each other. Baste around the top to hold the bag and lining securely together.

**7.** Sew the short ends of the drawstring casing pieces together with a 1˝ seam allowance. Leave a 1½˝ gap in the middle of the seams for the cord. Turn each seam allowance under ½˝ to hem, and sew in place.

Sew the casing.

**8.** Sew the casing to the top edge of the bag, with right sides facing and the casing seams in the middle of the sides.

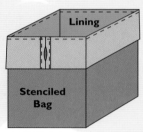

Attach the casing to the bag.

**9.** Turn ¼˝ under on the raw edge of the casing and press. Fold the casing over to the inside of the bag. Sew in place.

Turn under ¼˝ and fold to inside. Sew.

**10.** Thread the drawstring through the casing. Decorate the drawstring and bag as desired.

Tassel made from cotton made in Elin Noble's thread dyeing workshop

Drawstrings made from leather thongs and completed with handmade beads made from recycled glass by Ronel Visser

*Silly Birds Bag.* Designed, stenciled, and painted by Pam Stallebrass and hand embroidered and beaded by Des van Niekerk. Stencil patterns are on page 66.

This beautiful old quilt, or *ralli*, from Pakistan was the inspiration and starting-off point for the quilt project presented in this chapter. This quilt was appliquéd, but we are going to print the design through a freezer-paper stencil. Photo courtesy of John Gillow.

The cutwork appliqué on this quilt from Pakistan inspired me to cut some shapes from folded paper. I started off trying to find out how the blocks in the Pakistani *ralli* were folded and cut, then I tried different variations. It was great fun, and I found I could create all sorts of designs in this way. I then folded freezer paper in the same way and cut the designs into it for the blue colorway (page 31). This then became my stencil.

Folding and cutting is commonly used in Pakistani *rallis* and Hawaiian quilts, but fabric is used instead of a stencil. Be inspired by their designs and start off by copying them, then add your own variations. If you ruin a piece of paper, just throw it away. Keep on cutting new pieces until you are happy with the results, then transfer your design to freezer paper and fold, cut, and print. It's an easy way to be creative and original.

Designed, stenciled, pieced, and hand quilted by Pam Stallebrass.
Photo by Peter Steltzman.

I used a range of tones of blue, green, and blue-black for this quilt. The stencil is printed with quite a dark turquoise blue on white. The zigzag edge integrates the design quite well into the piecing. I love simple blocks like the Nine-Patch, so here we use a Nine-Patch in a Nine-Patch. The quilting incorporates machine and hand quilting.

- Quilt size: $78\frac{1}{2}" \times 78\frac{1}{2}"$
- Block size: $9" \times 9"$
- Borders: $2\frac{1}{2}"$ and $9"$
- Stencil method: One-color freezer-paper stencil

Please read the chapters on Stenciling (pages 10–15) and Paints, Dyes, and Paint Sticks (pages 16–18).

## Materials and Supplies

*Fabric requirements are based on 42" fabric width. See pages 10–12 for more information on supplies.*

- $1\frac{1}{2}$ yards of white for the stenciled blocks
- $\frac{1}{8}$ yard each of 28 fabrics in various greens, blues, and grays for the Nine-Patch blocks
- $3\frac{1}{4}$ yards of deep blue-green for the Double Nine-Patch blocks and outer border
- $\frac{2}{3}$ yard of green for the inner border
- $\frac{3}{4}$ yard of blue for binding
- Batting: $82" \times 82"$
- Backing: $82" \times 82"$
- Freezer paper
- Fabric paint (thickened dyes, fabric paints, or paint sticks): Turquoise blue
- Stencil brush, $\frac{1}{4}"$ to $\frac{1}{2}"$ in diameter

## Stenciling

### Cutting Fabric to Stencil

*The stenciled pieces will be trimmed to size before sewing. Extra width and length have been allowed.*

**WHITE**

✦ Cut 4 strips $10" \times$ the fabric width, then cut into 16 squares $10" \times 10"$.

**Making the Stencils**

1. Cut a 9" square from freezer paper. Fold it in half.

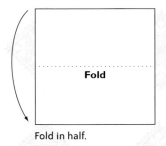

Fold in half.

2. Fold in half again to form a square.

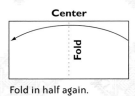

Fold in half again.

3. Fold the lower right-hand corner over to the upper left-hand corner to form a triangle.

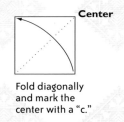

Fold diagonally and mark the center with a "c."

4. Trace one of the patterns (pages 84–91) and place it on the folded triangle, making sure that the center of the design is in the center of the folded paper and that the zigzags are on the outside edge.

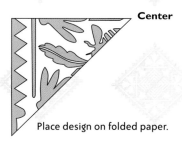

Place design on folded paper.

**5.** Cut out the design with small sharp scissors through all layers at once. All the shapes to be cut are on the edges, so you will not need a craft knife. Open it to see the full design. Repeat for each of the 16 stencil designs.

Cut out and open.

### Printing the Stencils

**1.** Press each stencil firmly onto a square of white fabric.

**2.** Stencil the designs with turquoise blue, varying the tone from light to dark on each piece for interest.

Block detail

**3.** Heat set following the instructions on page 15.

**4.** Trim the blocks to $9\frac{1}{2}\,''\times 9\frac{1}{2}\,''$, centering the design.

## Nine-Patch Blocks and Borders

### Cutting

**VARIOUS GREENS, BLUES, AND GRAYS**

✦ Cut 45 strips $1\frac{1}{2}\,''\times$ the fabric width for the small Nine-Patch blocks.

**DEEP BLUE-GREEN**

✦ Cut 6 strips $3\frac{1}{2}\,''\times$ the fabric width, then cut into 64 squares $3\frac{1}{2}\,''\times 3\frac{1}{2}\,''$.

✦ Cut 2 strips $5\frac{1}{2}\,''$, then cut into squares $5\frac{1}{2}\,''\times 5\frac{1}{2}\,''$. Cut twice diagonally for the side triangles. Also cut 2 squares $3\,''\times 3\,''$, then cut in half diagonally for the corner triangles.

✦ Cut 8 strips $9\frac{1}{2}\,''\times$ the fabric width for the outer border.

**GREEN**

✦ Cut 6 strips $3\,''\times$ the fabric width for the inner border.

### Nine-Patch Blocks

Sew the $1\frac{1}{2}\,''$ strips into the following sets. Make each set 5 times, trying for as many different combinations as you can.

Nine-Patch blocks

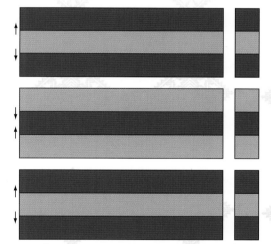

Join $1\frac{1}{2}\,''$ strips. Press. Trim ends, then cut into $1\frac{1}{2}\,''$ units.

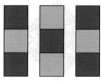

Arrange units.

Stitch, matching seams. Press. Make 105 in as many different combinations as you can.

## Assembling the Quilt Top

1. Referring to the diagrams, arrange the Nine-Patch blocks and the deep blue-green squares, side triangles, and corner triangles. Make 9 center blocks, 12 side blocks, and 4 corner blocks.

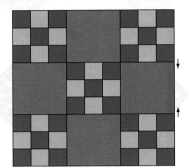

Double Nine-Patch blocks

2. Join the Nine-Patch and stenciled blocks into diagonal rows.

3. Trim the selvages from the inner border strips and sew into 1 long length.

4. Measure the quilt top from top to bottom through the center and cut 2 inner border strips this length. Add to the sides of the quilt top and press.

5. Measure the quilt top from side to side through the center and cut 2 inner border strips this length. Add to the top and bottom of the quilt top and press.

6. Repeat Steps 3–5 to join, measure, cut, and add the outer borders.

## Finishing

I used light-sensitive paints and leaves to print the backing fabric (page 15). It's great to get the family involved in this process.

Layer, baste, and quilt.

Hand quilt the stenciled blocks from corner to corner with a blue variegated embroidery cotton. Then quilt the border with zigzags, and the triangles using a variegated teal embroidery thread. I used the same thread to outline a plant form in the borders.

Bind with blue fabric (pages 61–62).

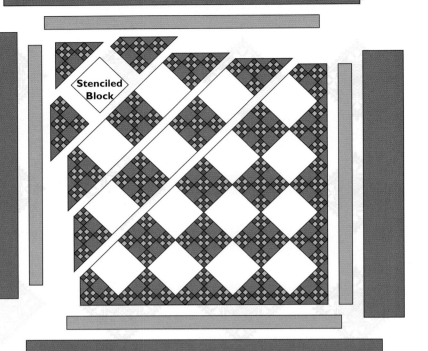

Quilt top construction

*Bees and Elephants—Autumn Shades.* Designed, dyed, stenciled, pieced, and hand quilted by Pam Stallebrass. Photo by Peter Steltzman.

# Agapanthus

My mother always loved the blue of the agapanthus flowers. I wanted the blue, almost purple, of these flowers to be the main feature of this quilt. The green balances the purples, and the mix of the two colors gives a softer variation of both colors and creates some lovely dull lavender hues and dirty greens.

There is only one stencil to cut, and detail is added after one layer of paint has been applied. It is quite time consuming, and a bit like a cross between stenciling and fabric painting.

There are nine big blocks. The flower is stenciled in the center, and various widths of strips are added to the corners, so when the blocks are joined it looks as if the strip-pieced blocks are on point.

Designed, stenciled, and pieced by Pam Stallebrass and machine quilted by Beverley Patterson.
Photo by Peter Steltzman.

A blue-purple was the starting point for the color scheme. When you look at a bed of flowering agapanthus, the blue is surrounded by green blade-like leaves. We are going to mix a variety of blues and purples, then mix the green and blue-purple together to make sludgy greens and dirty purples.

Only one stencil is cut for this design. A basic blue is painted on, then detail is added in a darker color.

Machine quilting in the ditch holds the three layers together, and a little hand quilting is done on the flowers. I added a few purple-green beads to the centers of a few of the flowers.

- Quilt size: $72\frac{1}{2}'' \times 72\frac{1}{2}''$
- Block size: $18'' \times 18''$
- Border: $9''$
- Stencil method: A single stencil with hand-painted details

Please read the chapters on Stenciling (pages 10–15) and Paints, Dyes, and Paint Sticks (pages 16–18).

## Materials and Supplies

*Fabric requirements are based on 42" fabric width. See pages 10–12 for more information on supplies.*

- 5 yards of white for the stenciled blocks and border block foundations
- $\frac{1}{4}$ yard each of 45 different blues, purples, and greens in dark and light shades for the pieced blocks
- $\frac{5}{8}$ yard of purple for binding
- Batting: $76'' \times 76''$
- Backing: $76'' \times 76''$
- Freezer paper or stencil plastic
- Fabric paints: Turquoise, magenta, and clear base
- Watercolor brushes, $\frac{1}{2}''$ and $\frac{1}{4}''$

## Stenciling

### Cutting Fabric to Stencil

*The stenciled pieces will be trimmed to size before sewing. Extra width and length have been allowed.*

#### WHITE

✦ Cut 9 squares $19'' \times 19''$. Only the center will be printed; the rest will be covered with strip piecing.

### Making the Stencil

**1.** A quarter of the pattern is shown with the octagonal frame around it (page 64). Take your chosen stencil material and draw a line through the center from top to bottom, then another at right angles from side to side. Trace the design into each of the 4 segments to make up the whole flower.

Complete stencil

**2.** Cut out the design with a craft knife. Cut around the octagon; it will help you later when you start the piecing.

## Printing the Stencil

**1.** Fold your fabric in half and score the fold with your finger, then fold again to establish the center. Line up the stencil center with the fabric folds and pin in place. If you are using a freezer-paper stencil, iron it, pressing firmly to stick the stencil to the fabric.

Fold, score, then fold again to establish the center. Center stencil, pin, and iron.

Mixed colors

**2.** Paint the blue-purple randomly over the flowers.

Paint the blue-purple.

**3.** Add pinkish-purple and blue-purple to complete the first layer. Keep these colors very pale.

Add pinkish-purple and blue-purple.

**4.** With the stencil still in place, draw a darker line of blue-purple down the center of each petal and smooth it off with your finger or a dry brush.

Add darker line down petal centers.

**5.** With the stencil face down, carefully peel the fabric from the stencil. This stops the paper from curling, so it is easier to use again.

Remove stencil.

**6.** Center the design in the octagonal frame and mark it with a water-soluble pen or a pencil.

Center in octagonal frame and mark.

## Blocks and Border

### Cutting

#### WHITE

✦ Cut 7 strips 10″ × the fabric width, then cut into 28 squares 10″ × 10″ for the border block foundations.

#### GREENS

✦ Cut 4 strips 1½″ × the fabric width from each of 9 of the greens for the stenciled block borders.

✦ Cut 18 squares 5″ × 5″ from the same green fabrics as above. Cut in half diagonally for the corners of the stenciled blocks.

✦ Cut the rest of the green fabric into strips of varying widths from 1″ to 1¾″ for the blocks and border.

#### PURPLES AND BLUES

✦ Cut into strips of varying widths from 1″ to 1¾″ for the blocks and borders.

### Agapanthus Blocks

**1.** Place the 4 green half-square triangles on the corners of the stenciled blocks. Stitch and press open.

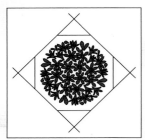

Triangle placement

Place half-square triangles.

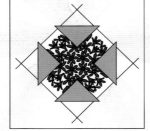

Stitch and press open.

**2.** Place 2 of the 1½″ green strips as shown. Stitch, trim, and press. Add the other two 1½″ green strips. Stitch, trim, and press.

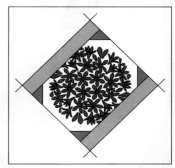

Add the first 2 strips.

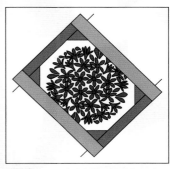

Add the next 2 strips.

Stitch and press open.

**3.** Randomly place and stitch varying widths of purple, blue, and green strips to fill the foundations. Make 9 blocks.

Block construction

**4.** Trim the blocks to $18\frac{1}{2}'' \times 18\frac{1}{2}''$.

Agapanthus block

### Border Blocks

Place the strips diagonally across the blocks, and stitch varying widths of purple, blue, and green strips to fill the foundations. If you prefer, place the blues and greens mostly on one half of each block to make a zigzag effect on the edges of the quilt. Make 28 blocks. Trim the blocks to $9\frac{1}{2}'' \times 9\frac{1}{2}''$.

Border block

## Assembling the Quilt

Referring to the diagram, arrange and join the blocks and border blocks.

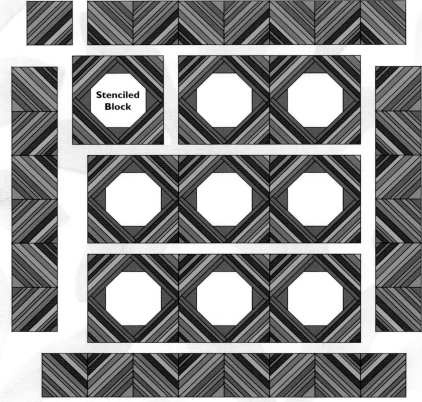

Quilt top construction

## Finishing

Layer, baste, and quilt.

Machine quilt, stitching in the ditch.

Bind with purple fabric (pages 61–62).

Color option: Dark purple fabric paint on a light purple background

Color option: Opaque pearl lilac on a deep purple background

# Butterflies

Butterflies from the Amazon forests that inspired these designs

My family was asked to look after a farm for two weeks by friends who were attending their son's wedding. I decided to work on the butterfly quilt while I was there, but forgot to pack my freezer paper and the Markal crayons that I had bought especially for the project. I searched the local shops for materials and found some acetate and spray adhesive at the stationery shop, and tiny bottles of fabric paint at a craft shop.

I used one stencil for the basic shape, and a second on top of the first for extra detail. Both the tropical (page 42) and blue (page 57) colorways use a Log Cabin variation to frame the motifs, one with triangles and the other with pineapple piecing. Both are done on a paper foundation. It is so exact and neat, and once you have done a few it is really very easy.

Designed, stenciled, and pieced by Pam Stallebrass, machine quilted by Beverley Patterson, and hand quilted by Pat Thorne.

I wandered around the farm garden that we were house-sitting. The vegetation was semitropical, and the colors were wonderfully fresh and bright. I picked a selection of red, orange, and pink flowers, and mixed fabric paints to match them.

I repeated the butterfly colors in the triangles of the Log Cabin and used black to emphasize the jewel colors. Most of the quilting is in the ditch, but we had a bit of fun in the border with variegated cotton. Details in the butterfly wings were highlighted with hand quilting.

The butterflies were printed on a coarse cotton fabric. I chose this because of the texture (a contrast to fine muslin) and because it looked like counted-stitch cloth, and I wanted to add embroidery stitches to the wings for added color and texture. It is really easy to print on coarse fabric; you don't have to be too careful about adding too much color at a time and having the color bleed under the stencil. I like to slosh on the paint, so it turned out to be a good choice.

- Quilt size: 73″ × 89½″
- Block size: 15½″ × 15½″
- Sashing: 1″
- Borders: 2½″ and 8½″
- Stencil method: Stencils with layered color

Please read the chapters on Stenciling (pages 10–15) and Paints, Dyes, and Paint Sticks (pages 16–18).

## Materials and Supplies

*Fabric requirements are based on 42″ fabric width. See pages 10–12 for more information on supplies.*

- ¾ yard of pastel coarse cotton for the stenciled butterflies
- ¼ yard each of 12 fabrics in warm and bright tones of gold, terra-cotta, orange, red, maroon, and purple for the blocks
- 4¾ yards of black for the blocks and sashing
- ¾ yard of red-orange for the inner border
- 2⅓ yards of black for the outer border
- ¾ yard of maroon for binding
- Batting: 77″ × 93″
- Backing: 77″ × 93″
- Stencil plastic
- Spray adhesive
- Fabric paints: Magenta, yellow, turquoise, and clear base to lighten the colors
- Stencil brush, ¼″ to ½″ in diameter
- Transparent tape

## Stenciling

### Cutting Fabric to Stencil

*The stenciled pieces will be trimmed to size before sewing. Extra width and length have been allowed.*

**PASTEL**

✦ Cut 3 strips 8″ × the fabric width, then cut into 12 squares 8″ × 8″.

### Making the Stencils

There are 5 butterfly patterns (pages 67–71), and each has 2 stencils, except for #4, which has 3. The complete wing shape is painted first in a very light color. The darker shaded portions are the second stencil. Below each pattern is a diagram showing the separate stencils. It is important to trace the whole outline of the butterfly onto the second stencil so you know exactly where to place it. Make the stencils 6½″ × 6½″.

Butterfly 1a and b

Butterfly 1a

Butterfly 1b

### Printing the Stencils

**1.** Spray the back of stencil 1a with adhesive and let dry for a few minutes.

**2.** Place it carefully on the center of your fabric square and use a pencil to mark around the outside edge of the square; this is your cutting line.

**3.** Print the first stencil in a very light color. Shade the color as you wish to add interest. Let dry, then remove the stencil.

**4.** Spray the back of stencil 1b with adhesive and let dry for a few minutes.

**5.** Place it over the stenciled design, lining up the traced design with the shape of the wings.

**6.** Add a medium-toned color for the detail on the wings.

**7.** When it is dry, iron to set the color.

The first color in stencil 1

The second color in stencil 1

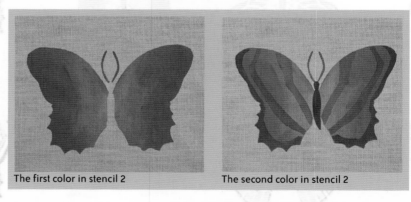

The first color in stencil 2

The second color in stencil 2

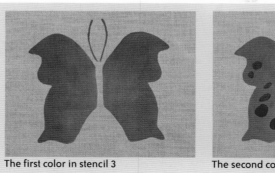

The first color in stencil 3

The second color in stencil 3

The first color in stencil 4     The second and third colors in stencil 4

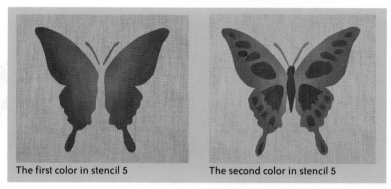

The first color in stencil 5     The second color in stencil 5

**8.** Repeat these steps for all the butterflies. Make a few extra so you have a variety to choose from for your project. Trim the blocks along the penciled lines; they should be 6½″ × 6½″.

25 different butterflies. There are 5 different designs made in 5 colorways.

## Blocks and Borders

### Cutting

#### WARM AND BRIGHT COLORS

✦ Cut 12 strips 1⅜″ × the fabric width for the colored frames around the butterflies. From the strips, cut 4 pieces for each block, 2 each of 7″ and 9″ lengths. *These pieces are cut oversize for paper piecing.*

✦ Cut 20 squares 1½″ × 1½″ for the sashing squares.

✦ Cut 12 strips 3½″ × the fabric width, then cut into squares 3½″ × 3½″. Cut in half diagonally to make half-square triangles. Each block needs 16, for a total of 192. Cut a few extra. *These pieces are cut oversize for paper piecing.*

#### BLACK

✦ Cut 68 strips 2″ × the fabric width for the Log Cabin strips. From the strips, cut 16 pieces for each block, 4 each of 8½″, 10½″, 12½″, and 14½″ lengths. *These pieces are cut oversize for paper piecing.*

✦ Cut 16 strips 1½″ × the fabric width, then cut into 1½″ × 16″ pieces for sashing. Cut 31 pieces.

✦ Cut 8 strips 9″ × the fabric width for the outer border.

#### RED-ORANGE

✦ Cut 7 strips 3″ × the fabric width for the inner border.

## Block Construction

**1.** For each block, trace or photocopy the paper-piecing pattern (page 72) 4 times, then tape the copies together to make a 15½″ block. Add a ¼″ seam allowance around the outside edge. Add the numbers, as they show the order to add the fabric pieces. Draw seamlines in the corners of the butterfly frame (pieces 2–5). Make 12 patterns.

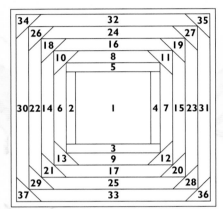

Paper-piecing pattern

**2.** Place the paper foundation on a light table (or up against a window) and carefully center the butterfly design on the blank side. Pin in place.

Center and pin.

**3.** Select one of the 1⅜″ × 7 strips for the butterfly frame. Align it with the #2 strip on the pattern and pin in place. With the right side of the paper up, stitch on the line between #1 and #2. Press open. Trim off the excess strip.

Pin frame strip.

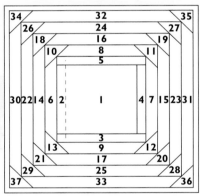

Stitch.

Press open.

**4.** Repeat for pieces #3–#5.

**5.** Next, take the 2″ black strips and sew them in place (pieces #6–#9).

**6.** Take 4 triangles of the same color and add these next (pieces #10–#13).

**7.** Repeat Steps 5 and 6 with the longer black strips and different colored triangles to complete the block. Carefully tear away the paper from each block.

**8.** Trim each block to 16″ × 16″.

## Assembling the Quilt Top

**1.** Referring to the diagram, arrange and join the blocks and sashing.

**2.** Trim the selvages from the inner border strips and sew into 1 long length.

**3.** Measure the quilt top from top to bottom through the center and cut 2 inner border strips this length. Add to the sides of the quilt top and press.

**4.** Measure the quilt top from side to side through the center and cut 2 inner border strips this length. Add to the top and bottom of the quilt top and press.

**5.** Repeat Steps 2–4 to join, measure, cut, and add the outer borders.

Stenciled Block

Quilt top construction

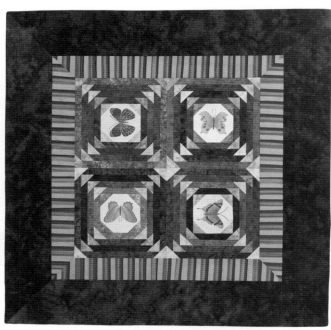

*Butterfly Sampler.* Unfinished quilt top designed, stenciled, and pieced by Pam Stallebrass.

## Finishing

The blocks are quilted in the ditch by machine. The black border can be quilted by hand or machine. We used a variegated thread, making a diamond design with a butterfly in each.

Pat Thorne highlighted the detail on the butterfly wings with hand quilting using embroidery thread. A guide for these lines can be seen on the stencil patterns on pages 67–71.

Bind with maroon fabric (pages 61–62).

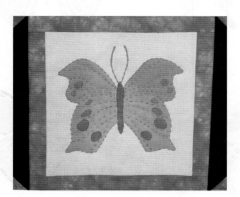

Yellowwood
Tree

Designed and stenciled by Pam Stallebrass and sewn and quilted by Pat Thorne.
Photo by Peter Steltzman.

It's funny, and sometimes frustrating, when a quilt has a mind of its own. This quilt was going to be a fairly traditional floral quilt. The floral blocks and the pieced blocks looked as if they were going to work, but when I did the yellow-wood border, it overwhelmed the whole design. My design wall hangs in the dining room so I can look at it all the time, and I asked my son, Matthew, what he thought. He suggested I get rid of the floral blocks. I was horrified; I had spent so much time on them! Still, I took them off, and immediately it looked much better. Now I needed something much simpler to replace them. Again, Matthew came to the rescue. He twirled the piece of the yellowwood twig I had been drawing around his finger, and it made an almost perfect circle. Voilà! I decided to print this wreath a paler color for two reasons. In the spring this dark green tree produces a pale green sprig of leaves from the end of each branch; and for design reasons, it would have been boring to have too much of the same shade and strength of blue. I really only wanted the central blocks to provide a suggestion of the leaves—a guide to quilting.

I had been experimenting with light-sensitive paints and found that black plastic, cut with scissors and placed on top of the wet paint, gave a good image. I liked the idea of a pale leaf on a dark background, so I thought I would give it a try with this design. The slight variation in each print gives it a nice organic feeling.

This is a project for those people who tell me they can't draw. You just have to cut out some black plastic and drip some color on the fabric. It couldn't be easier!

You could also use real leaves with your light-sensitive paints. Or, freezer paper could be used as a stencil, ironed in place, and the background filled in with fabric paints and a stencil brush.

- Quilt size: $76\frac{1}{2}'' \times 76\frac{1}{2}''$
- Block size: $16'' \times 16''$
- Borders: $1\frac{1}{2}''$, $10\frac{1}{2}''$, and $2''$
- Stencil method: Black plastic templates and light-sensitive paint

Please read the chapters on Stenciling (pages 10–15) and Paints, Dyes, and Paint Sticks (pages 16–18).

## Materials and Supplies

*Fabric requirements are based on 42″ fabric width. See pages 10–12 for more information on supplies.*

- $3\frac{3}{4}$ yards of white for the square and rectangular stenciled blocks
- $\frac{1}{4}$ yard each of 28 to 40 light to dark green fabrics and light to medium-dark purple fabrics for the pieced blocks and pieced border
- 1 yard of dark purple for the inner border and binding
- Batting: $80'' \times 80''$
- Backing: $80'' \times 80''$
- 100-micron black plastic for the stencil (or similar dark, thick, flexible plastic that you can cut with scissors)
- Spray adhesive
- Tracing paper
- Light-sensitive paint: Blue, purple, and green
- Small plastic squeeze bottles or pipettes for dripping dye
- Stiff plastic for portable work surface

## Stenciling

### Cutting Fabric to Stencil

*The stenciled pieces will be trimmed to size before sewing. Extra width and length have been allowed.*

**WHITE**

✦ Cut 4 squares $18'' \times 18''$ for the interior blocks.

✦ Cut 14 rectangles $12'' \times 20''$ for the borders.

### Making the Stencil

**1.** Trace the leaf wreath and border leaf patterns (pages 92–97) onto tracing paper. Glue them temporarily onto the plastic with spray adhesive.

**2.** Cut out the stencils with scissors. They are very floppy, but they are in one piece and can be arranged on a dry piece of fabric. I tried putting the wreath onto a damp piece of fabric and all the leaves stuck together and made it almost impossible!

### Printing the Stencil

**1.** Mix your colors with light-sensitive paint, and add water to lighten the colors. The square wreath blocks are much paler than the border blocks.

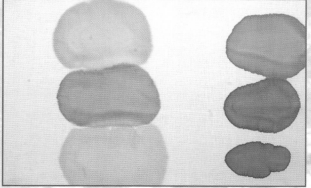

Mix greens and purples from your light-sensitive paints, adding water to lighten the colors.

**2.** Mark the final size of the squares ($16˝ \times 16˝$) and rectangles (6 rectangles $10\frac{1}{2}˝ \times 17˝$ for the side borders and 8 rectangles $10\frac{1}{2}˝ \times 18˝$ for the top and bottom borders).

**3.** Arrange the black plastic stencil on the dry fabric. I work on a piece of stiff plastic; it is light enough to carry around but firm and waterproof.

The black plastic shape cut from the center will help you arrange the template into the correct shape.

**4.** Spray water over the fabric and stencil to prevent hard edges from forming on the colors.

**5.** Drip little puddles of blue, purple, and green paint until there is no white fabric left showing. You want it to creep under the stencil.

After you have sprayed the fabric and template with water, drip on the mixed colors.

**6.** Slide your finger down each leaf shape to make sure it is pressed down onto the wet fabric. You can rearrange the leaves a little so they don't touch each other.

**7.** Leave the board in the sun until completely dry.

**8.** Carefully remove the stencil and iron the fabric to make sure it is dry where the stencil was, and to set the color.

Remove stencil and iron.

**9.** Repeat Steps 3–8 for the rest of the blocks, using the border leaf pattern (pages 96–97) on the rectangle pieces.

**10.** Trim the square blocks to $16\frac{1}{2}˝ \times 16\frac{1}{2}˝$ and the border rectangles to $11˝ \times 17\frac{1}{2}˝$ and $11˝ \times 18\frac{1}{2}˝$.

## Pieced Blocks and Borders

### Cutting

#### GREENS AND PURPLES

✦ Cut 80 pieces 8″ × 11½″ for quick-piecing the half-square triangles, or 3″ × 3″ squares cut in half diagonally (320 for the blocks and 148 for the border) for traditionally pieced half-square triangles.

## note
### make extra to give options in your layout.

#### DARK PURPLE

✦ Cut 5 strips 2″ × the fabric width for the inner border.

### Half-Square Triangle Unit Construction

The basic building block is the half-square triangle. I make the triangles larger than necessary, then trim them to size.

#### QUICK-PIECED HALF-SQUARE TRIANGLES

**1.** Pair a lighter and a darker 8″ × 11½″ fabric.

**2.** Draw six 3″ × 3″ squares on the lighter fabric, then draw diagonal lines as shown.

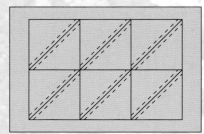

Draw the solid lines, sew on the dashed lines (¼″ from solid lines), and cut on the solid lines.

**3.** Sew ¼″ from the diagonal lines (the dashed lines in the diagram).

**4.** Cut on the solid lines to make 12 half-square triangle units. Repeat for all 8″ × 11½″ pieces. Press.

**5.** Trim each unit to 2½″ × 2½″, making sure the seamline is at the corners. You will need 468 units.

### TRADITIONALLY PIECED HALF-SQUARE TRIANGLES

**1.** Pair a lighter and a darker 3″ half-square triangle.

**2.** Stitch on the long side. Press.

**3.** Trim each unit to 2½″ × 2½″, making sure the seamline is at the corners. You will need 468 units.

### Block and Border Construction

The pieced blocks are 64-patch blocks made from the half-square triangle units. Have fun with these blocks. Model yours on these examples, or see how many variations you can come up with.

**1.** Piece 5 blocks.

Pieced block 1

Pieced block 2

Pieced block 3

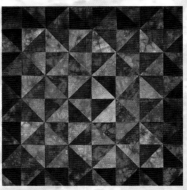

Pieced block 4

Pieced block 5

**2.** Sew half-square triangles into 4 long strips for the pieced borders—36 units for each side and 38 units for the top and bottom. Press.

### Assembling the Quilt Top

**1.** Referring to the diagram, arrange and join the stenciled and pieced blocks.

**2.** Trim the selvages from the inner border strips and sew into 1 long length.

**3.** Measure the quilt top from top to bottom through the center and cut 2 inner border strips this length. Add to the sides of the quilt top and press.

**4.** Measure the quilt top from side to side through the center and cut 2 inner border strips this length. Add to the top and bottom of the quilt top and press.

**5.** Add the stenciled border blocks.

**6.** Add the side pieced borders and press.

**7.** Add the top and bottom borders and press.

## Finishing

Layer, baste, and quilt.

Pat Thorne machine quilted in the ditch. Then she hand quilted down the center of each leaf in the central blocks and created a ribbon design in the stenciled border.

Bind with dark purple fabric (pages 61–62).

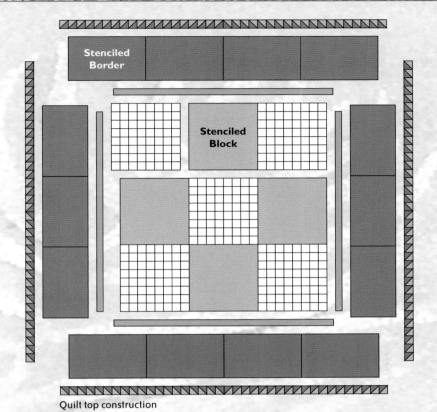

Quilt top construction

This colorway uses a silk-screened stencil rather than a template. The central blocks are stenciled in a very light gray-purple on a mottled mushroom/lavender-colored fabric, and the leaf border is stenciled in a deep gray-blue on the same color fabric.

*Spirit of the Yellowwood.* Designed, stenciled, pieced, and quilted by Pam Stallebrass. Photo by Peter Steltzman.

Quilt size: $84\frac{1}{2}" \times 84\frac{1}{2}"$

Block size: $16" \times 16"$

Sashing: $4"$

Border: $10" \times 20"$ blocks

This quilt is for my husband. Years ago I asked him to cook on Saturday nights to give me a break. What started out as a chore for him has now become an intense interest and a hobby that has expanded to include growing vegetables. The main stencil of each design was used to paint the black background. Then, after ironing to set the black, I hand painted the vegetables and herbs using detail stencils to get a good crisp line between some of the colors. These are indicated with numbers and letters on the patterns in the back of the book. Freezer paper was used for the pebble path in the sashing strips. Black fabric paint was applied with a sponge roller (page 13). For the herb blocks, I overlapped separate stencils.

Stencil patterns are on pages 98–111.

*The Veggie Patch.* Designed, stenciled, and pieced by Pam Stallebrass and machine quilted by Lorraine Bodie and Beverly Patterson.

Quilt size: $56\frac{1}{2}" \times 56\frac{1}{2}"$

Block size: $16" \times 16"$

Sashing: $4"$

Border: $6"$

For this quilt, I used only blues, greens, and purples. The colorway is very soft and restful. I used only the four herb blocks—tarragon, sage, marjoram, and rosemary—and left out the bay leaf border.

Stencil patterns are on pages 98–103 and 111.

*The Herb Garden.* Unfinished quilt top designed, stenciled, and pieced by Pam Stallebrass. Photo by Pam Stallebrass.

This jacket was made in a similar manner to the *Blue and White Leaves* quilt (page 20). I used 6″ blocks (2½″ strips for the Nine-Patches) instead of 7½″, and opaque ink (bronze in a pearl base) to outline the leaves, since the fabric was dark.

Stencil patterns are on page 81.

Back of *Autumn Leaf Jacket*. Designed, stenciled, pieced, and quilted by Pam Stallebrass. Photo by Peter Steltzman.

Quilt size: 42½″ × 42½″

Block size: 17″ × 17″

Borders: 1″, 3½″, 3″, and 5″

This quilt would make a lovely wedding gift because the oak represents durability, and because of the hearts quilted on the borders. I also thought it could be a family tree for a new baby, with the names of the child's ancestors and relations embroidered or written in each leaf. The central medallion is 17″ square (finished). The quilting on the outer border was inspired by traditional Welsh designs.

Stencil patterns are on pages 82–83.

*The Green Oak*. Designed, stenciled, pieced, and quilted by Pam Stallebrass. Photo by Peter Steltzman.

Quilt size: $22\frac{1}{2}'' \times 22\frac{1}{2}''$

Block sizes: $8'' \times 8''$ and $1'' \times 1''$

Border: $3''$

I used the smallest oak leaves I could find, and cut a very simple trunk and acorns from freezer paper. Using a teal green (blue with a dash of yellow and red) and a small stencil brush, I painted a halo around the templates on cross-stitch fabric (Aida). I filled in the leaf, branch, and acorn shapes with cross-stitch, using three strands of hand-dyed DMC embroidery thread. The cross-stitch areas were then outlined with one strand of dark green.

Stencil patterns are on page 83.

*Tree of Life*. Designed, stenciled, pieced, and quilted by Pam Stallebrass. Photo by Pam Stallebrass.

Quilt size: 60½″ × 60½″

Block size: 12″ × 12″

The butterflies are framed by pineapple Log Cabin blocks. Martie wanted to emphasize the subtle gradations of color, so the darker sections of each block go from light to dark. The strips in the light sections are randomly placed. There are four colors, each with a ten-color gradation.

Stencil patterns are on pages 67–71.

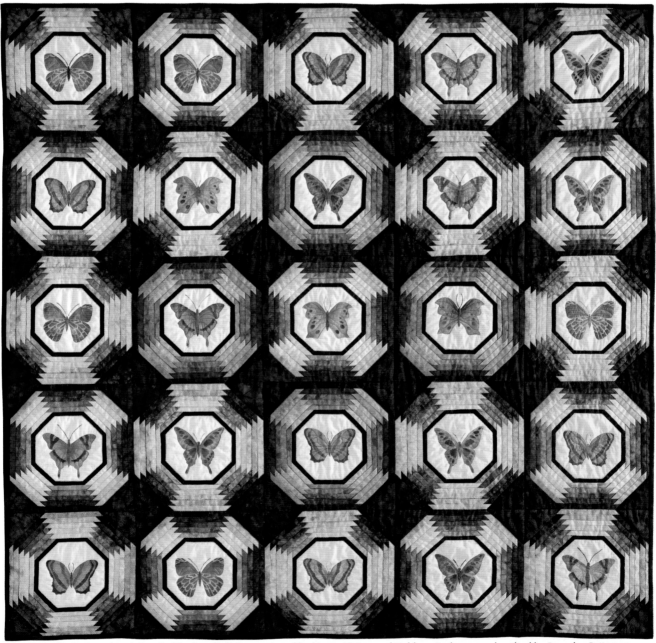

*Blue Butterfly*. Designed and stenciled by Pam Stallebrass, pieced by Martie McLea and Nohleen Berkman, and quilted by Beverley Patterson.

*Baby Elephants.* Designed, stenciled, pieced, and quilted by Pam Stallebrass. Photo by Pam Stallebrass.

Quilt size: 47½″ × 47½″

Block size: 9″ × 9″

Borders: 1″, 3″, and 6″

A simple Square-in-a-Square block was used for this wonderful quilt. Large leaves are quilted on the border using stranded, hand-dyed threads.

Stencil pattern is on page 65.

The back of the elephant quilt was painted with thickened Procion dyes (page 18).

A large fan-shaped leaf was used for the quilting design.

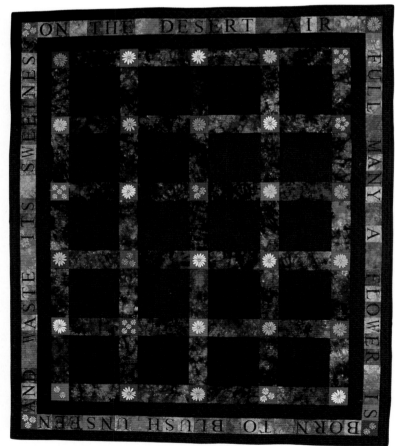

*Desert Secrets—Autumn Colorway.* Designed, stenciled, pieced, and quilted by Pam Stallebrass. Photo by Pam Stallebrass.

Quilt size: 52½″ × 62″

Block size: 7″ × 7″

Sashing: 2½″

Borders: 2″, 2¼″, and 1½″

The quilt is called *Desert Secrets* for both the flowers that "blush unseen" and the illusive, mystical San who left their wonderful paintings and petroglyphs in the desert regions of Namaqualand. The stenciled areas are very small and are located in the sashing blocks and in the border. The sashing is randomly dyed with rich autumn colors, and the letter border is dyed using the same colors but a shade lighter.

Stencil patterns are on page 111.

Strip-woven kente cloth from West Africa

*Mandela's Gold*. Designed, stenciled, pieced, and quilted by Pam Stallebrass.
Photo by Peter Steltzman.

Quilt size: 45½″ × 66½″

Block sizes: 5″ × 5″, 5″ × 7″, and 5″ × 9″

Border: ¾″

This quilt was inspired by the wonderful kente cloths of West Africa. Long narrow strips 2″ to 6″ wide are woven using warp- and weft-faced designs, giving them very distinctive vertical and horizontal stripes. The strips are then sewn together into large cloths that are worn on special occasions by both men and women.

Stencil patterns are on pages 73–77.

Quilt size: $61\frac{1}{2}'' \times 82\frac{1}{2}''$

Block size: $7\frac{1}{2}'' \times 7\frac{1}{2}''$

Border: $4''$

I wanted the colors to be bright and fresh, so I used primary and secondary colors. They are all so bold that it's surprising they work together, but the blues and jades introduce a more sober note. The muslin is dyed in one- and two-color gradations to create a subtle variation of each color. The stenciling is a bit fiddly, but each one is small, and the stencils are easy to cut from freezer paper. The piecing is very easy; we used a simplified Nine-Patch block set on point and a strip-pieced border.

Stencil pattern is on page 111.

*Spring*. Designed, stenciled, pieced, and quilted by Pam Stallebrass and bound by Ashley Germani. Photo by Peter Steltzman.

A ¼-inch seam allowance is used in all the piecing.

## Layering and Basting

Press the quilt top, making sure all the seam allowances are ironed to one side. Test iron your fabrics, since some will get shiny over the thicker layers of fabric, especially some purchased black fabrics; with these fabrics press only from the back or with a pressing cloth or Teflon sheet.

I've discovered a fusible batting by Hobbs that is 80% cotton and 20% polyester. You just iron the three layers together, and as you are working you can re-iron it if necessary. I still baste around the outside and use a few safety pins around the area I'm working on, but it saves a lot of basting.

Very wide fabric is available for backing your quilts, but a seam joining two narrower pieces is quite acceptable. If you are going to hand quilt, don't choose a very closely woven fabric such as percale, since it is difficult to pull the needle through.

Lay out the three layers on the floor or a large table and hand baste vertically and horizontally in parallel rows about 4″ apart. Many quilters use safety pins instead of basting.

## Quilting

Both hand and machine quilting change and improve the texture and feel of the quilt. I love the way quilting introduces texture to the plain areas and highlights detail in the stenciled areas.

Machine quilting with a walking foot is really useful for holding the three layers together before doing detailed quilting by hand or machine. If you stitch really close to the seam, the stitching is virtually hidden—quilting in the ditch. Sew slightly to one side of the seam on the side opposite the seam allowance.

Free-motion machine quilting is useful for outlining stenciled shapes. Lower your feed dogs, or reduce your stitch length to 0 and use your embroidery foot. I usually use an embroidery hoop for small areas of quilting; I find it easier to move the fabric around while holding the hoop (see page 57, *Blue Butterfly*, and page 55, *Autumn Leaf Jacket*).

I love the big borders around the quilts, where machine or hand quilting looks wonderful, repeating some of the stenciled motifs (see page 42, *Tropical Butterflies*, and page 31, *Bees and Elephants—Blue*).

Hand quilting takes time, but it is really worth the effort. If you allocate a certain amount of time every day, you will be surprised at how much progress you make. Get comfortable and listen to the radio or taped stories, and it becomes a lovely, relaxing part of your day.

## Double-Fold Straight-Grain Binding (French Fold)

**1.** Trim excess batting and backing from the quilt.

**2.** For a ¼″ finished binding, cut the strips 2″ wide and piece together with a diagonal seam to make a continuous binding strip.

**3.** Press the seams open, then press the entire strip in half lengthwise with wrong sides together.

**4.** With the raw edges even, pin the binding to the edge of the quilt a few inches away from the corner; leave the first few inches of the binding unattached.

**5.** Sew, using a ¼″ seam allowance.

**6.** Stop ¼″ away from the first corner (A) and backstitch one stitch. Lift the presser foot and needle. Rotate the quilt one quarter turn. Fold the binding at a right angle so it extends straight above the quilt (B). Then bring the binding strip down even with the edge of the quilt (C). Begin sewing at the folded edge.

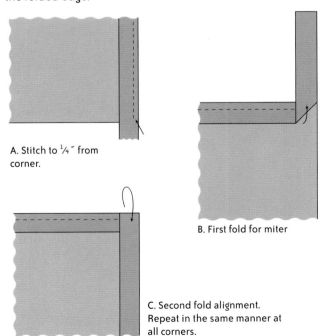

A. Stitch to ¼″ from corner.

B. First fold for miter

C. Second fold alignment. Repeat in the same manner at all corners.

### Finishing the Binding

**METHOD 1:**

Fold under the beginning end of the binding strip ¼˝. Lay the end of the binding strip over the beginning folded end. Continue stitching beyond the folded edge. Trim the excess binding. Fold the binding over the raw edges to the quilt back and hand stitch, mitering the corners.

**METHOD 2:**

Fold the ending tail of the binding back on itself where it meets the beginning binding tail. From the fold, measure and mark the cut width of the binding strip. Cut the ending binding tail to this measurement. For example, if the binding is cut 2˝ wide, measure from the fold on the ending tail of the binding 2˝ and cut the binding tail to this length.

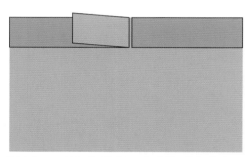

Fold, then cut binding tail to cut width of binding.

Open both tails. Place one tail on top of the other tail at right angles, right sides together. Mark a diagonal line and stitch on the line. Trim the seam to ¼˝. Press open. Finish sewing the binding to the quilt.

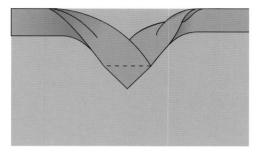

Stitch ends of binding diagonally.

Fold the binding over the raw edges to the quilt back and hand stitch, mitering the corners.

# About the Author

Pam's two passions are crafts and travel. After studying fine arts she travelled extensively in Europe. She returned home to South Africa and completed her studies to become an art teacher. After marrying, she and her husband decided to build a catamaran and sail around the world. They sailed across the Atlantic from Durban, South Africa, to Brazil. Sailing slowly northward, they travelled via the San Blas Islands and through the Panama Canal and eventually landed in Peru where they stayed for two years working on an irrigation project. While in Peru Pam studied the archaeology of the area and travelled to many of the archaeological sites. The colors of the ancient weavings found in the Paracas desert still influence her work.

While her two children were growing up she started a craft market in her hometown, Somerset West, which has become one of the best in South Africa, providing a platform for excellent craft work.

She lives near Cape Town and dyes and prints fabric, which she sells regularly at quilt shows in England, UK, and once at the International Quilt Festival and Market in Houston. She also volunteer teaches different crafts to disadvantaged teenagers because she feels that it will make a difference in their lives. Other members of the craft market are invited to do short courses such as glass bead making, card and felt making and pinhole photography.

She writes articles on quiltmaking for *British Patchwork and Quilting*. Her two previous books were *The South African Guide to Fabric Screen Printing*, published by Struik in South Africa and New Holland Press in the UK, and *Beadwork, a World Guide* (co-authored with Caroline Crabtree), published by Thames and Hudson in the UK, Rizzoli in the USA, and translated into French, German, and Japanese.

## Sources

*For more information, ask for a free catalog:*
C&T PUBLISHING
P.O. Box 1456
Lafayette, CA 94549
(800) 284-1114
email: ctinfo@ctpub.com
website: www.ctpub.com

*For quilting supplies:*
COTTON PATCH MAIL ORDER
3405 Hall Lane, Dept. CTB
Lafayette, CA 94549
(800) 835-4418
email: quiltusa@yahoo.com
website: www.quiltusa.com

PRO CHEMICAL AND DYE
P.O. Box 14
Somerset, MA 02726
(800) 2-BUY-DYE
website: www.prochemical.com

PATCHWORK & QUILTING MAGAZINE
Traplet Publications
Traplet House, Pendragon Close
Malvern, Worcestershire UK WR14 1GA
(UK) 1684 588500
Fax: (UK) 1684 578558
email: customerservice@traplet.com
website: www.pandqmagazine.com

# Stencil Patterns

Note: The stencil material is white and the cutaway areas are gray.

Complete stencil

*Agapanthus* (page 36), quarter of stencil

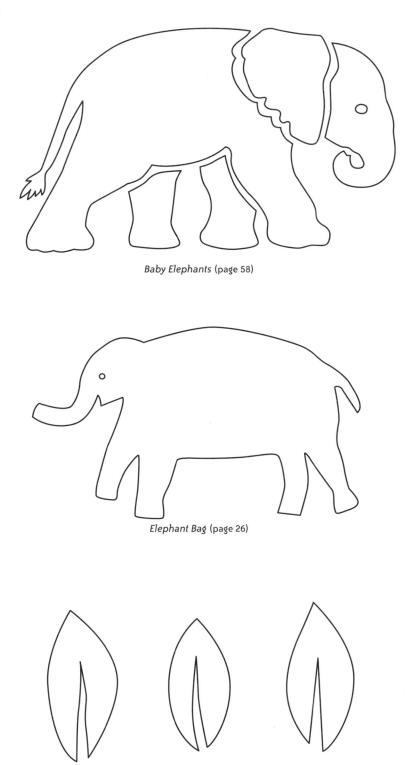

*Baby Elephants* (page 58)

*Elephant Bag* (page 26)

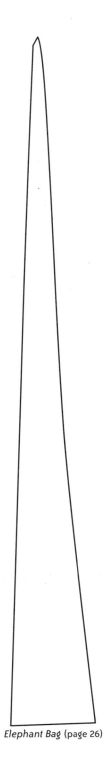

*Elephant Bag* (page 26)

*Elephant Bag* (page 26)

*Silly Birds Bag* (page 29)

*Silly Birds Bag* (page 29)

*Silly Birds Bag* (page 29)

*Blue Butterfly* (page 57) and *Tropical Butterflies* (page 42), Butterfly #1

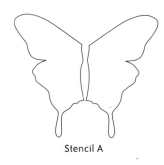

Stencil A

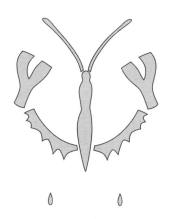

Stencil B

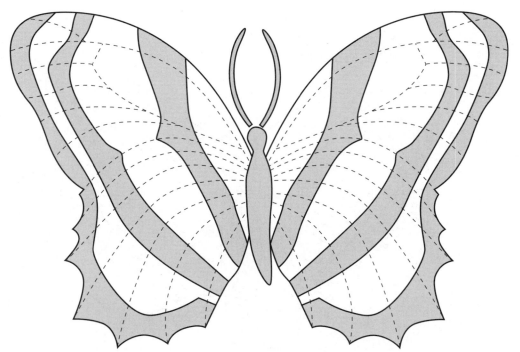

*Blue Butterfly* (page 57) and *Tropical Butterflies* (page 42), Butterfly #2

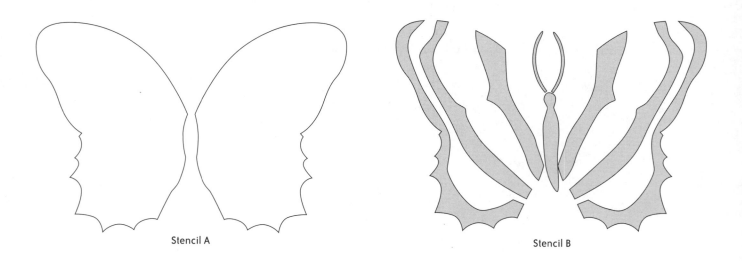

Stencil A

Stencil B

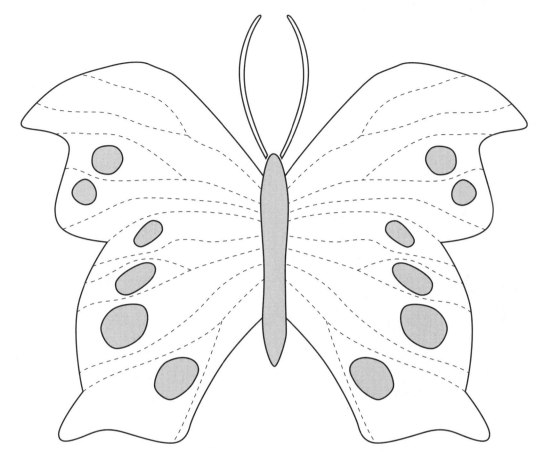

*Blue Butterfly* (page 57) and *Tropical Butterflies* (page 42), Butterfly #3

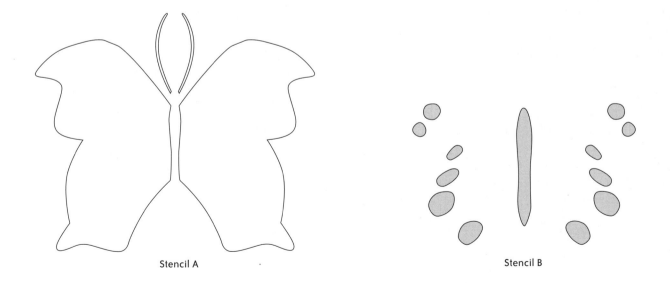

Stencil A

Stencil B

*Blue Butterfly* (page 57) and *Tropical Butterflies* (page 42), Butterfly #4

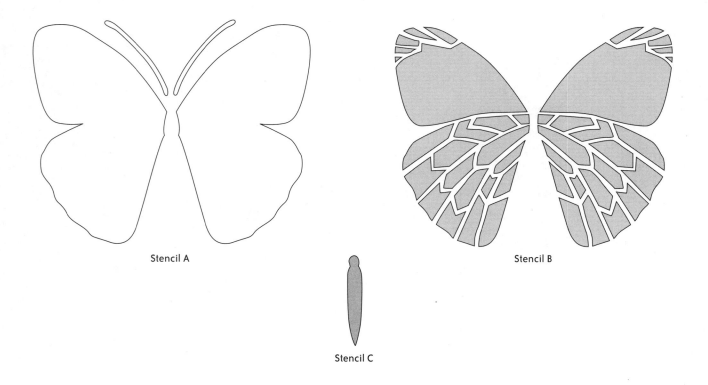

Stencil A

Stencil C

Stencil B

*Blue Butterfly* (page 57) and *Tropical Butterflies* (page 42), Butterfly #5

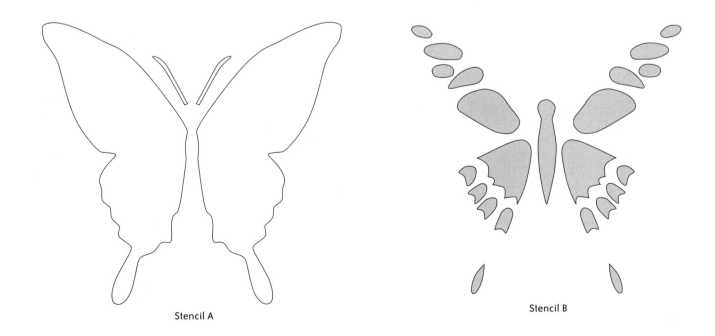

Stencil A

Stencil B

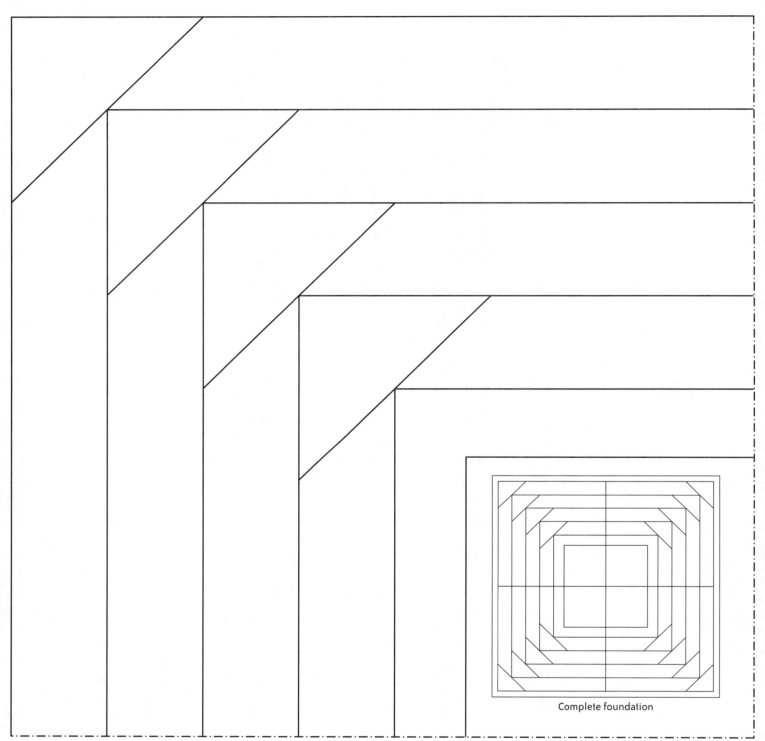

Complete foundation

*Tropical Butterflies* (page 42), quarter of foundation

Umbrella, *Mandela's Gold* (page 59)

Horseman, *Mandela's Gold* (page 59)

Bird, *Mandela's Gold* (page 59)

Warrior, *Mandela's Gold* (page 59)

Hat, *Mandela's Gold* (page 59)

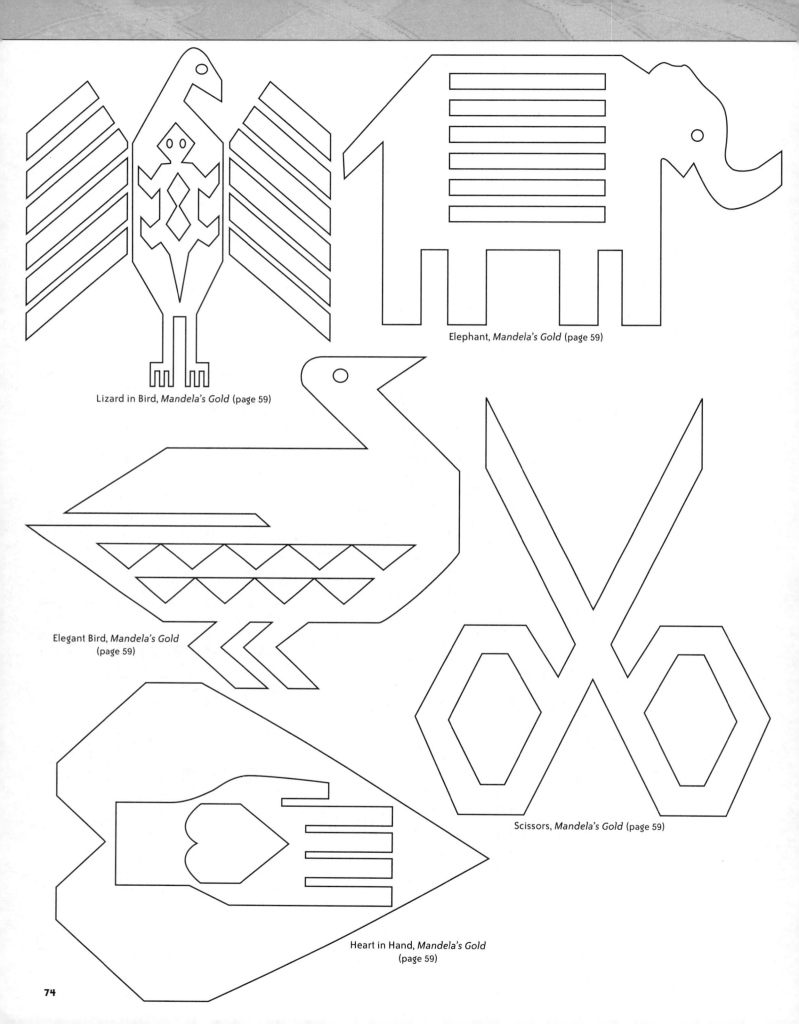

Lizard in Bird, *Mandela's Gold* (page 59)

Elephant, *Mandela's Gold* (page 59)

Elegant Bird, *Mandela's Gold*
(page 59)

Scissors, *Mandela's Gold* (page 59)

Heart in Hand, *Mandela's Gold*
(page 59)

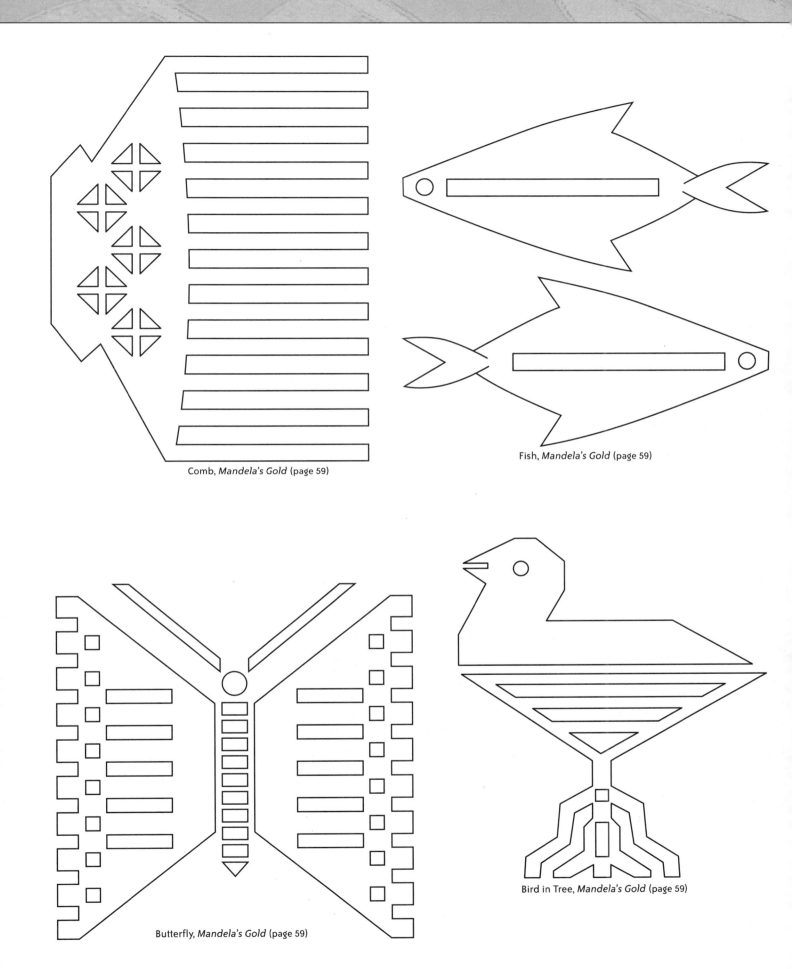

Comb, *Mandela's Gold* (page 59)

Fish, *Mandela's Gold* (page 59)

Butterfly, *Mandela's Gold* (page 59)

Bird in Tree, *Mandela's Gold* (page 59)

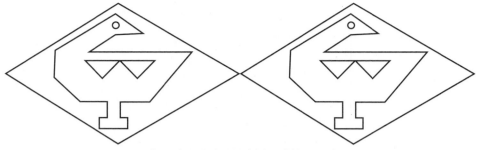

Birds Looking Back, *Mandela's Gold* (page 59)

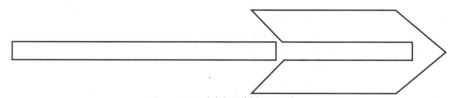

Spear, *Mandela's Gold* (page 59)

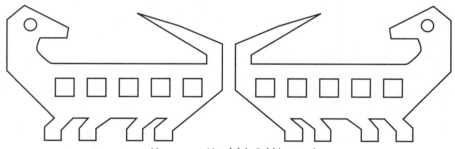

Mongooses, *Mandela's Gold* (page 59)

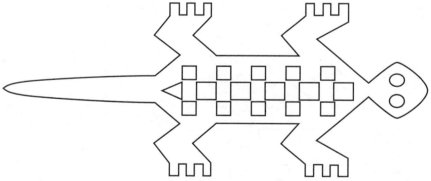

Lizard, *Mandela's Gold* (page 59)

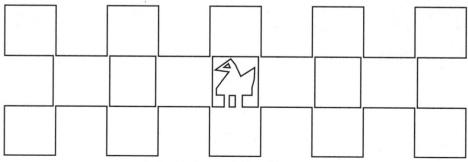

Bird in Blocks, *Mandela's Gold* (page 59)

Chevron Border, *Mandela's Gold* (page 59). Note: The dotted line is the edge of the block, but it is easier to trim and join your blocks later if you stencil the area that goes into the seam allowance. Stencil half the blocks with orange/yellow/orange zigzags and half with yellow/orange/yellow.

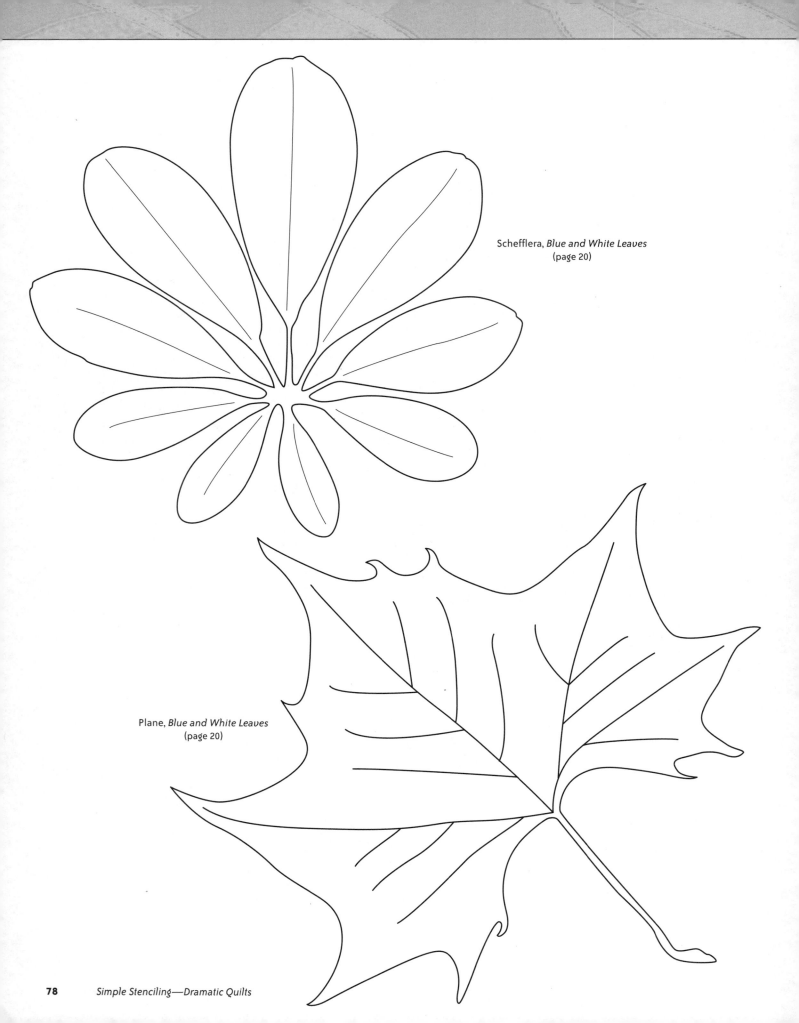

Schefflera, *Blue and White Leaves*
(page 20)

Plane, *Blue and White Leaves*
(page 20)

*Ivy, Blue and White Leaves* (page 20)

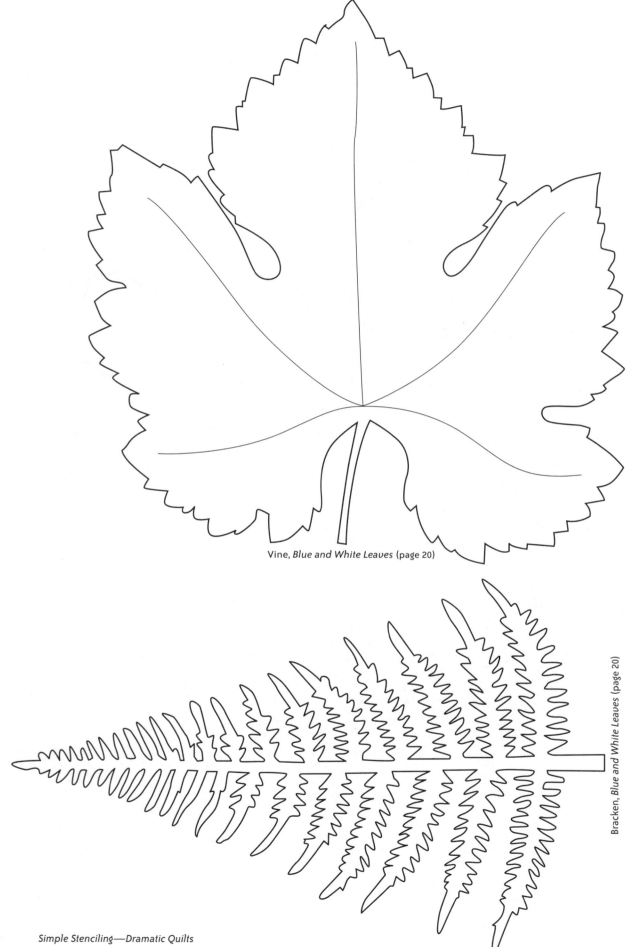

Vine, *Blue and White Leaves* (page 20)

Bracken, *Blue and White Leaves* (page 20)

Pin Oak Leaves, *Autumn Leaf Jacket* (page 55)

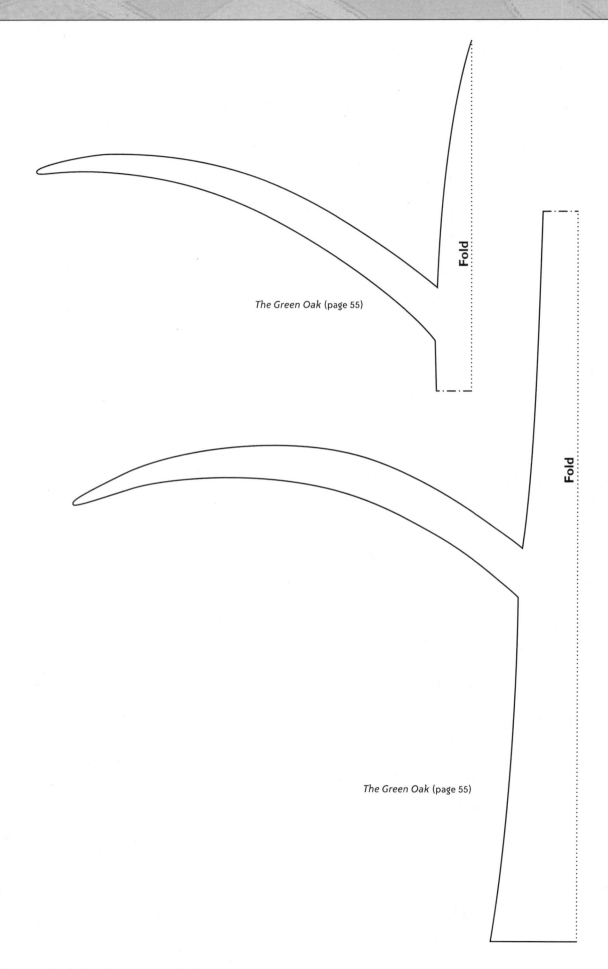

*The Green Oak* (page 55)

**Fold**

*The Green Oak* (page 55)

**Fold**

Oak Leaves and Acorns, *The Green Oak* (page 55)

*Tree of Life* (page 56)

**Center**

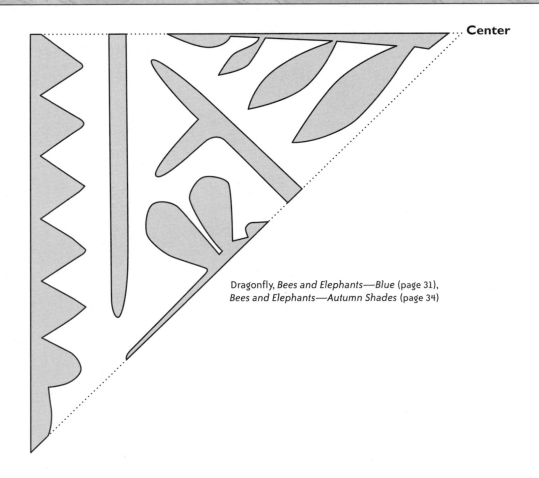

Dragonfly, *Bees and Elephants—Blue* (page 31),
*Bees and Elephants—Autumn Shades* (page 34)

**Center**

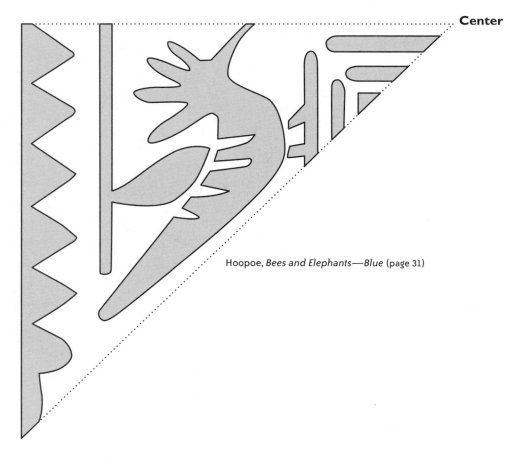

Hoopoe, *Bees and Elephants—Blue* (page 31)

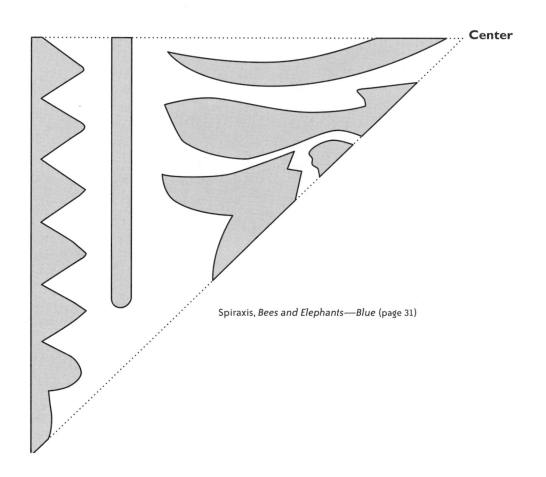

**Center**

Spiraxis, *Bees and Elephants—Blue* (page 31)

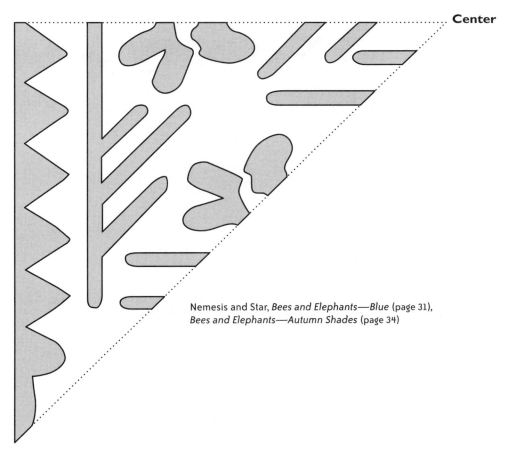

**Center**

Nemesis and Star, *Bees and Elephants—Blue* (page 31),
*Bees and Elephants—Autumn Shades* (page 34)

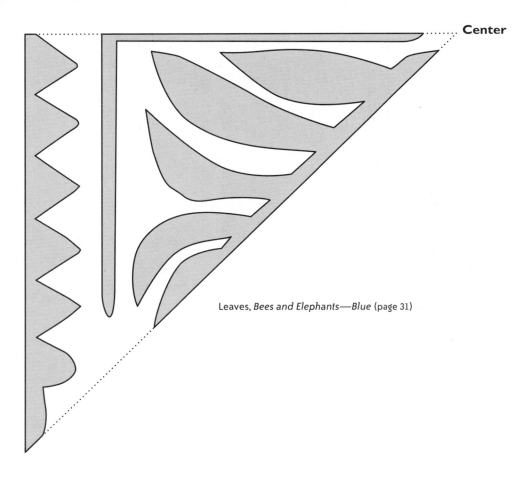

**Center**

Leaves, *Bees and Elephants—Blue* (page 31)

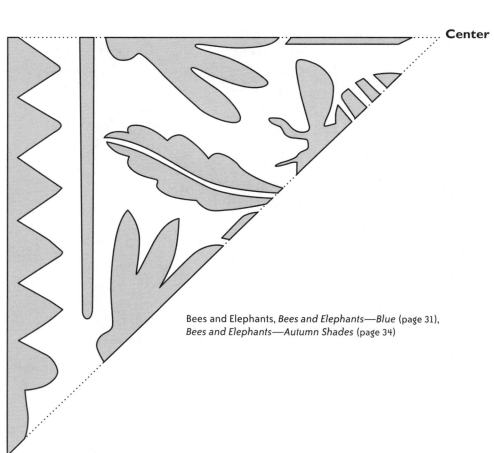

**Center**

Bees and Elephants, *Bees and Elephants—Blue* (page 31),
*Bees and Elephants—Autumn Shades* (page 34)

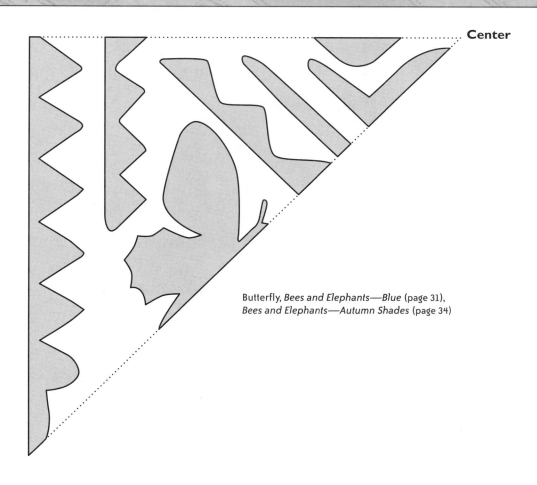

**Center**

Butterfly, *Bees and Elephants—Blue* (page 31),
*Bees and Elephants—Autumn Shades* (page 34)

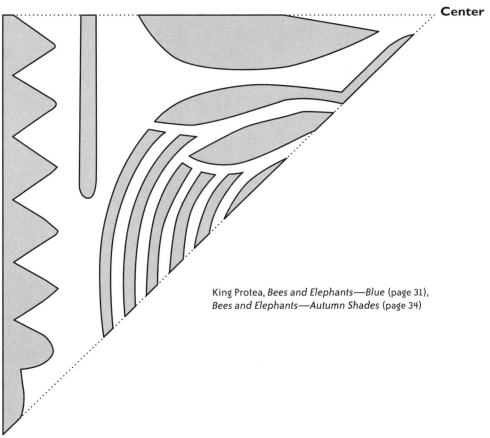

**Center**

King Protea, *Bees and Elephants—Blue* (page 31),
*Bees and Elephants—Autumn Shades* (page 34)

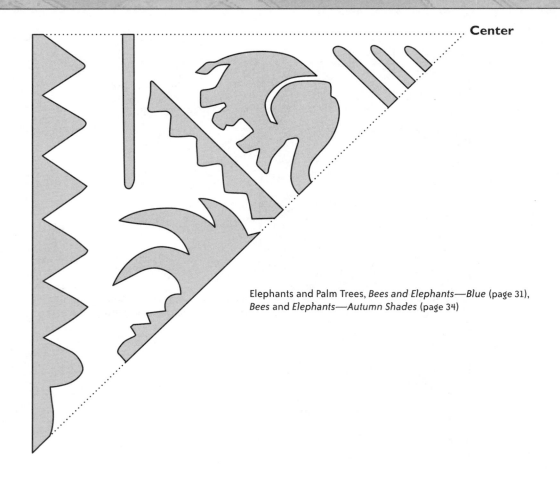

**Center**

Elephants and Palm Trees, *Bees and Elephants—Blue* (page 31),
*Bees* and *Elephants—Autumn Shades* (page 34)

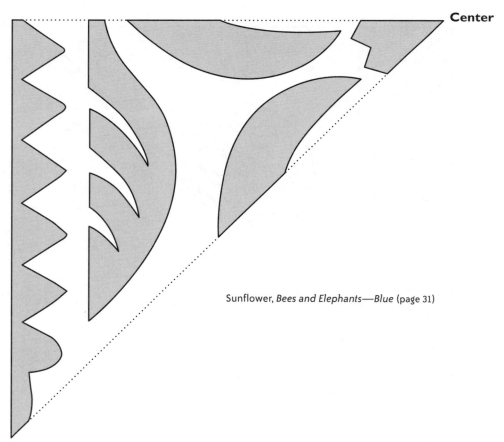

**Center**

Sunflower, *Bees and Elephants—Blue* (page 31)

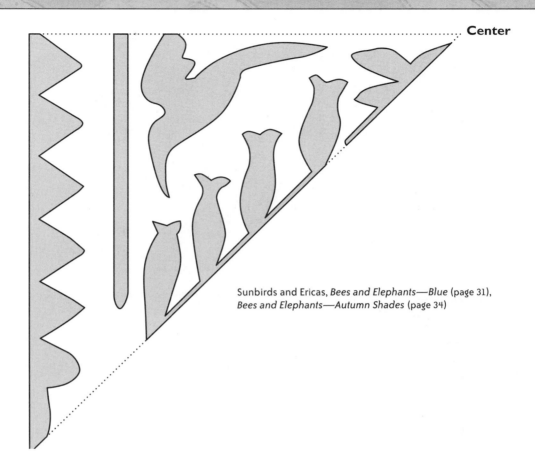

**Center**

Sunbirds and Ericas, *Bees and Elephants—Blue* (page 31),
*Bees and Elephants—Autumn Shades* (page 34)

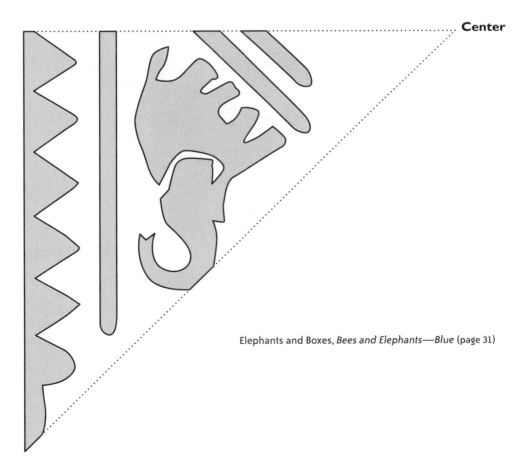

**Center**

Elephants and Boxes, *Bees and Elephants—Blue* (page 31)

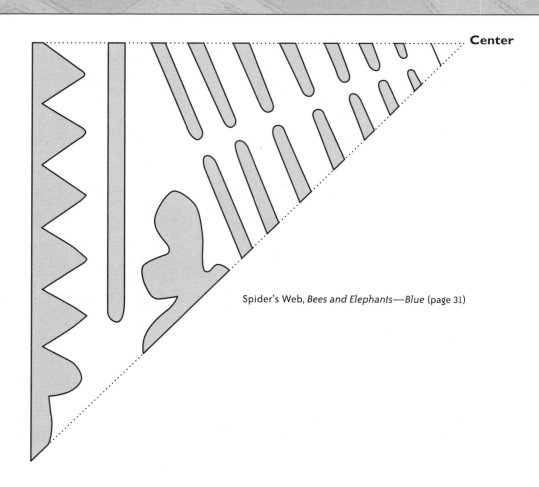

**Center**

Spider's Web, *Bees and Elephants—Blue* (page 31)

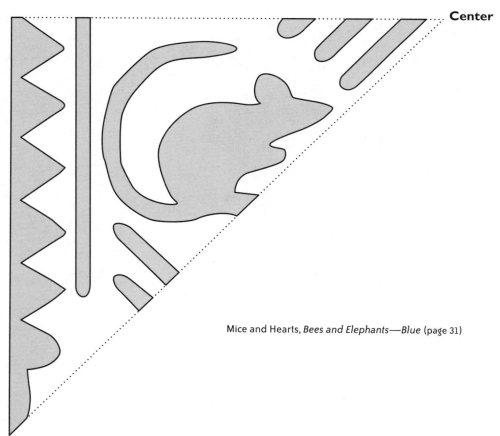

**Center**

Mice and Hearts, *Bees and Elephants—Blue* (page 31)

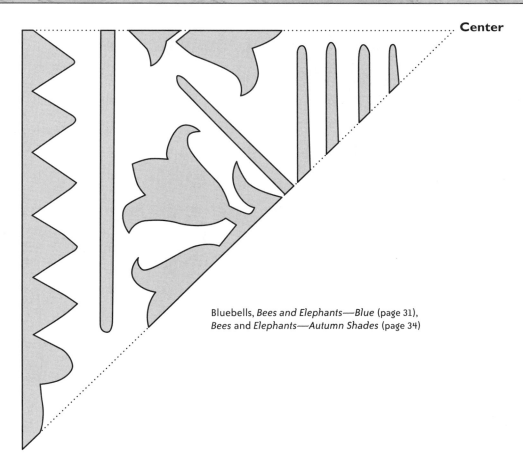

Bluebells, *Bees and Elephants—Blue* (page 31),
*Bees* and *Elephants—Autumn Shades* (page 34)

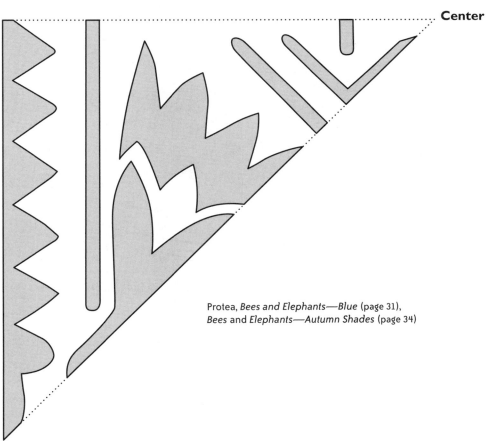

**Center**

Protea, *Bees and Elephants—Blue* (page 31),
*Bees* and *Elephants—Autumn Shades* (page 34)

*Nymph of the Evergreen Woodland* (page 49), *Spirit of the Yellowwood* (page 53),
Leaf Wreath, quarter #1

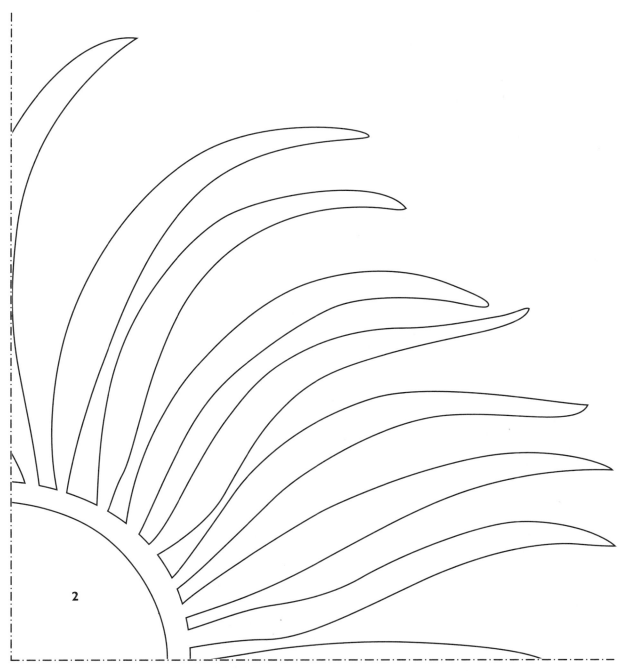

2

*Nymph of the Evergreen Woodland* and *Spirit of the Yellowwood,*
Leaf Wreath, quarter #2

**3**

*Nymph of the Evergreen Woodland* and *Spirit of the Yellowwood*,
Leaf Wreath, quarter #3

*Nymph of the Evergreen Woodland* and *Spirit of the Yellowwood*,
Leaf Wreath, quarter #4

Complete Leaf Wreath

*Nymph of the Evergreen Woodland* (page 49) and *Spirit of the Yellowwood*, (page 53) Border Leaf, half #1

*Nymph of the Evergreen Woodland* and *Spirit of the Yellowwood*, Border Leaf, half #2

Complete Border Leaf

Marjoram, *The Veggie Patch* (page 54), *The Herb Garden* (page 54)

Rosemary, *The Veggie Patch* (page 54),
*The Herb Garden* (page 54)

Sage, *The Veggie Patch* (page 54),
*The Herb Garden* (page 54)

Sage, *The Veggie Patch* (page 54),
*The Herb Garden* (page 54)

Tarragon, *The Veggie Patch* (page 54),
*The Herb Garden* (page 54)

Tarragon, *The Veggie Patch* (page 54),
*The Herb Garden* (page 54)

Aubergine (Eggplant), *The Veggie Patch* (page 54)

Ornamental Gourds, *The Veggie Patch* (page 54)

Fig, *The Veggie Patch* (page 54)

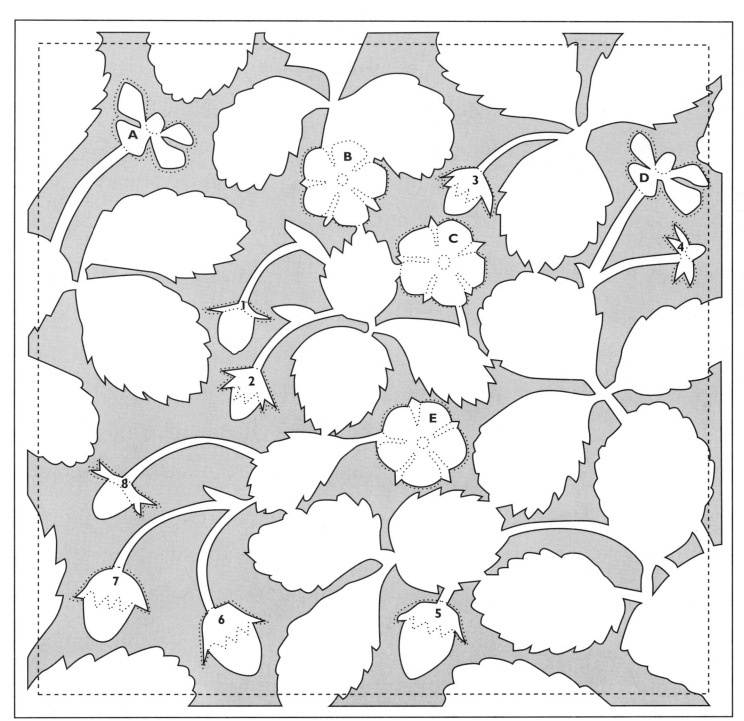

Strawberry, *The Veggie Patch* (page 54)

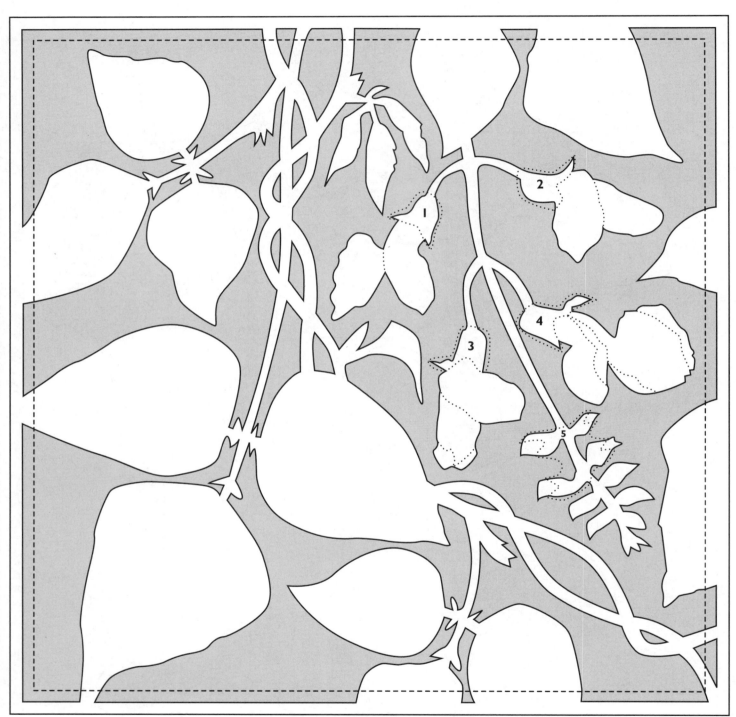

Runner Bean, *The Veggie Patch* (page 54)

Bay Leaf, *The Veggie Patch* (page 54)

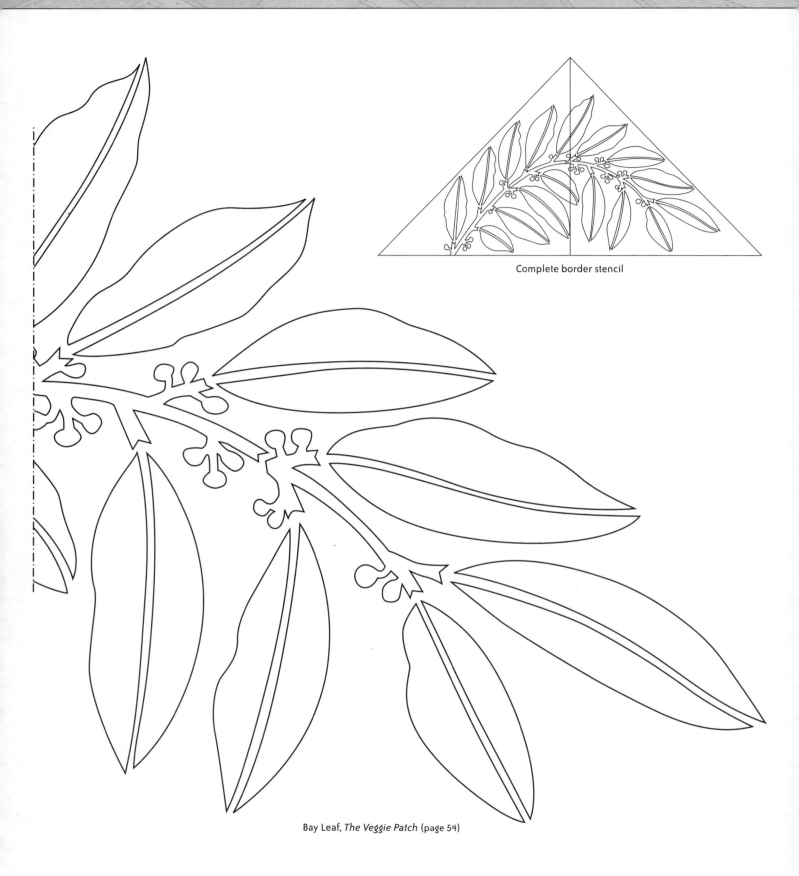

Complete border stencil

Bay Leaf, *The Veggie Patch* (page 54)

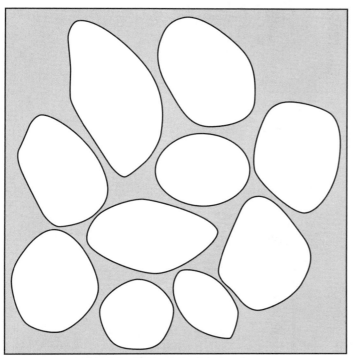

Pebble Path, *The Veggie Patch* (page 54),
*The Herb Garden* (page 54)

*Spring* (page 60)

*Desert Secrets—Autumn Colorway* (page 58)

*Desert Secrets—Autumn Colorway* (page 58)

# Great Titles
## from

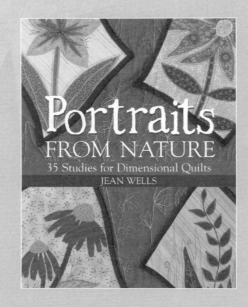